DIVORCE

IS THE PITS

So Stop Digging

SUCCESS STRATEGIES FOR PARENTS

By

Dr. Thomas Muha, Ph.D. • Dr. Maureen Vernon, Ph.D.

Looking Glass Productions, Inc.

ACKNOWLEDGEMENTS

We extend our appreciation to our families for their patience and support. This project could only have been accomplished with their love and understanding.

We would like to thank our colleagues who helped review our manuscript. Our special thanks goes to Dr. Jeffrey Barnett for the time he devoted and his many useful suggestions.

This project could not have been completed without the dedication and excellent assistance that was provided by Debra Hampton, M.S.W. We will always be grateful to her for helping us realize this goal.

Cover Art: Robert Howard Graphic Design, 631 Mansfield Drive, Ft. Collins, CO 80525

Graphic Design: Words & Pictures, Inc., 27 South River Road South, Edgewater, MD 21037

Printing: BookCrafters, 613 E. Industrial Drive, Chelsea, MI 48118-0370

Library of Congress Catalog Card 95-078498

ISBN 0-9647334-2-0

When one door of happiness closes
another one opens.
But often we look so long at the closed door
that we do not see the one that has opened for us.

We must all find these open doors,
and if we believe in ourselves,
we will find them and make ourselves
and our lives as beautiful as God intended.

Helen Keller

TABLE OF CONTENTS

PREFACE

As clinical psychologists who teach people how to better cope with life's problems, we've come to understand the importance of working through problems. It's our experience that you cannot make your life better by just reading about it, complaining about it, or crying about it. You have to *DO* something about it.

We have written and designed this book to give you both the information you need and the opportunity to apply what you are learning to your life. While we can't provide individualized psychotherapy to you, we can give you the therapeutic exercises that have produced positive results for so many of the people that we have counseled.

This book is laid out with all of the left hand pages giving you information that you'll need to deal with your divorce. The right hand pages provide a variety of ways for you to apply that information to your life. In some parts you'll already know what you want to do, and you can easily complete the exercise. Other areas will require some extra attention, and you'll want to work on the exercise until you make the breakthrough that will get what you need. You'll find it's easy to work with the book in short spurts as time permits.

By applying the things you will learn to your life, you can give yourself a much needed gift during the crisis created by your divorce. In China, crisis is written by combining two characters — one for danger and another for opportunity. Your life can be better than it has ever been if you take advantage of the opportunity to complete the exercises in this book and then follow through by implementing what you will learn into your life.

FOREWORD

F or so many families divorce has come to represent a way of life rather than the rare exception it was once. For millions of parents and their children it has turned their lives upside down, creating lives filled with unanswered questions, unmet needs, broken promises and broken hearts.

Divorce has reached epidemic proportions in America. It has become the scourge of a generation. From roots which valued hard work, teamwork and cooperation we have become a disposable society.

For too many the motto has become "if it's broken, throw it out." Rather than learn to work out problems and resolve differences, far too many parents have walked away from unhappy marriages only to find themselves forced to deal with many of the same issues — even more unhappy than before.

When a marriage fails and parents divorce the emotional fallout is significant. It is a traumatic experience for all involved. It is a decision that has a devastating impact on parents and children alike. The irony of it all is that for the benefit of their children parents must learn to achieve in divorce all that they were unable or unwilling to do when married — much of which actually led to the divorce. As coparents they must learn to communicate, resolve problems, work together and not use their children as weapons.

For most this is a very difficult challenge. Without clear guidance they are destined to repeat the same mistakes that led to the divorce. This book provides that clear guidance. Drs. Muha and Vernon have developed a step-by-step approach that helps parents to successfully overcome these challenges.

Divorce is the Pits, So Stop Digging offers numerous invaluable lessons, each followed by practical exercises which will assist parents in making the necessary changes so that the emotional mine field of divorce can be successfully navigated.

Drs. Muha and Vernon provide clear explanations and helpful suggestions. Most importantly, they help individuals to get past the anger, resentment, and pain so that parents and children can move on to a productive, healthy and happy life.

While not trying to replace counseling, which for many is an important part of the process, this book will likely prove to be an invaluable resource to the many thousands who truly need what it offers: sound, clear, and useful advice; assistance in working through difficult emotions; and practical guidance on how to move on with life in a healthy manner.

Jeffrey E. Barnett, Psy.D.
Licensed Psychologist
Clinical Assistant Professor
Departments of Psychiatry and Pediatrics
University of Maryland School of Medicine

DIVORCE STATISTICS

- 50% of couples who marry for the first time will be divorced in 10 years.
- 60% of all second marriages will also end in divorce.
- Over 1 million children *each* year experience their parents' divorce:
    - 25% of those children will be high school drop-outs.
    - 40% will receive psychological help.
    - 65% never build a good post-divorce relationship with their fathers.
    - 30% never build a good post-divorce relationship with their mothers.
- Compared to people who have grown up with both parents in the home, adult children of divorce are 59% more likely to have problems in their own marriages.

DIVORCE EDUCATION AND RESULTS

- Parents who learn how to handle their divorce experience go to court significantly less often over custody and visitation issues.
- Over 60% of parents who learn about dealing with divorce say that the information will help them to understand their children and will influence their behavior.
- Parents report a substantial reduction in tension and conflict with the other parent after conflict resolution training.
- When parents disentangle themselves from past problems, they're free to build a successful new life.

Survivors Of The "Pits" Speak Out

FRAN:

I couldn't believe how terrified and depressed I was when he finally left. I knew things had been pretty bad for a long time. But when he left it was like a part of me died. At first I wasn't able to take care of myself and so I wasn't much help to the kids either. Fortunately my therapist recommended this book, which helped me learn how to regain a feeling of power and control in my life.

JOHN:

She left and took the kids, and I didn't even know where they were staying for a week. When she did call, I was so angry that I wanted to crawl through the phone and shake some sense into her. How could she do this to me and the kids? We were headed for an all out custody battle, which would have ruined us financially and emotionally. The court ordered us to go to a mediator, and that turned out surprisingly well. We watched a video which taught us how to solve our problems.

SALLY:

At first I thought the children should spend time with their father. But then they came back talking about their father's girlfriend. I had hoped that he'd finally start spending time with the kids. I tried to talk to him about it, but he just got really defensive and we had some ugly scenes in front of the kids. A friend told me about this group for divorcing parents. The things I learned helped me to handle things much better than before. After all, we'll have to deal with each other about the children for years to come.

SAM:

After I left, my son Jason just seemed to fall apart. He stopped doing his school-work. He wasn't even interested in participating in sports the way he used to. He wasn't getting along at home or at school. I didn't understand what was going on until I read about how kids react to divorce. I learned a lot about how to help Jason adjust to our new living arrangement. He's back on track now and our relationship has even improved as a result of all of this.

CHAPTER 1

An Excavation Guide For "Hole" Climbers

Facing Divorce and Finding the Strength and Vision to Rebuild Your Life

NTRODUCTION

Divorce is the pits. It's a journey down into a hole so deep that for a long time you don't know where the bottom is. It's a hole so dark that you are bound to stumble and fall as you grope around trying to find your way out. You can feel lost and confused in a place that is dirty, cold and frightening.

How did your life end up in the pits? You started life's journey with such high hopes when you got married. The wedding was bright and beautiful, a peak experience. The dream was to share your life with someone who pledged to love, honor and respect you "Till Death Do Us Part."

Then the stress and strain of life began to pull the marriage apart. There was too much to do as you tried to take care of your partner, your children and yourself. Now, alone in a dark hole called divorce, you're left with horrible thoughts of ugly scenes: Being blamed for all of the problems . . . Sad scenes of the separation . . . Heart breaking images of your children's faces as they realized that their world was being destroyed.

The problems are unrelenting even now. The fights with your Ex continue over assets, custody, child support, visitation and on and on. You keep fighting back, trying to dig your way out from under all of the problems. It seems like you are in a tunnel, and that the harder you dig the sooner you'll break through to the other side. But instead, your life just seems to be going down deeper into the pits.

This book is dedicated to you. We know how hard you are trying, and we want to help guide your efforts towards getting to a good life. After all, you deserve it. What you need to get there is a guidebook that will give you the directions for what you can do to create the kind of life you have always wanted. If you are willing to make the effort, you can be like thousands of other people that we have helped to get their life out of the pits and onto solid ground.

- Chapter 1 will help you develop an understanding of how your life got into the pits. You'll learn about The First Law of Pit Holes: If your life is in the pits, stop digging, and figure out where you want to be.
- Chapter 2 is devoted to helping you know what it is you need in order to be happy. You'll have the opportunity to learn how to manage stress and refocus on your priorities.
- Chapter 3 will explore the feelings you're having about being stuck in the pits. And you'll learn how to stop feelings from flooding your thinking and creating another pitfall.
- In Chapter 4, you'll learn to use the SOLVE method to resolve conflicts with your Ex. Won't that be nice to know!
- In Chapter 5, you'll develop the skills you need to deal with resolving some specific problems involving your children, money, and relationships in your life.
- Chapters 6 and 7 are devoted to teaching you how to help your children come through the divorce in good shape.

You can learn to get your life back on track, and help your children to do that as well. *Congratulations!* You have started on your journey to a better life.

My Purpose In Reading This Book

Write down what you want to get from reading this book and completing the exercises:

_____

_____

_____

_____

_____

_____

_____

_____

_____

_____

_____

_____

_____

_____

_____

_____

_____

_____

_____

_____

_____

DIVORCE IS THE PITS

D ivorcing is much like cleaning up a toxic waste dump. Everybody denies having contributed to the contamination in the first place, and they want somebody else to clean up the mess. The fight over the clean up only poisons the environment even more than before. Often the results are disastrous. Many of the people involved in the process are exposed to such high levels of toxins that they never fully recover their health and well-being.

How in the world did you ever get to such a bad place in your life? When you got married, you probably didn't think that it would end in a bitter divorce battle. In fact, you very likely thought just the opposite — you were perfect for each other, madly in love and destined to share life as soul mates.

But something went terribly wrong. Instead of getting the love you needed, your partner betrayed you . . . neglected you . . . abandoned you. And it hurt you like nothing else has ever hurt you. It was like you had a big hole carved out of your insides. You felt lonely, hurt, sad, angry, and helpless to do anything about it.

Now you are in the process of divorcing: Contemplating it, starting the separation, struggling with the legal and emotional complexities, or trying to get your new life started. It isn't easy. You're desperately searching for answers about how you and your children can survive the divorce without the crippling effects that often occur.

We wrote this book to help you and your children have a happy and healthy life, after divorce. We have each gone through our own divorces. More importantly, we've helped thousands of families learn what they needed to do in order to go on to build a successful lifestyle for themselves. We've learned through our struggles, and those of our clients, some important lessons about what it takes to be able to create a good life.

David's Story

D avid's life seemed pretty tragic when he first came to counseling. His wife had moved out of their marital home and taken the two children with her. He reluctantly shared the fact that he had been having an affair. His wife had talked to him about their problems, but he never figured she'd leave him. David felt ashamed, angry and abandoned. If she really cared about their family, why didn't she hang in there instead of filing for a separation? Whenever he tried to talk to her about seeing the kids they ended up screaming and hanging up the phone on one another.

David was able to change things after learning that taking control of the situation meant taking control over his own behavior. He discovered he'd been following the same patterns of relating that he'd seen his father use in dealing with his mother.

David learned new ways to resolve the conflicts with his ex-wife by using the strategies in our SOLVE model. The exercises gave him the chance to practice positive communication patterns. He and his coparent have established a relationship in which they share a goal of raising two healthy kids. He now has a regular visitation schedule with his children, who are doing well.

MY PIT

**Draw a picture of your pit. Is it deep? Dark?
Filled with quicksand? Mud?**

Tom's Story

We had gone away on a vacation to the islands, but I was still miserable. If I can't be happy with this person even on a vacation, I thought to myself, then there's no chance for this marriage to work. So I said I wanted a divorce. My marriage of 17 years was going through its death throes.

I wanted to end the unhappiness, but things got worse before they got better. I replaced angry exchanges with my wife with anxious encounters with women I began to date. I exchanged the depression that was associated with feeling trapped in my marriage for the loneliness that accompanies separation.

I didn't think I would miss my wife after we separated, but I thought about her frequently. I thought a divorce would rid me of the frustration and anger that I was experiencing in my life. I discovered that it merely transferred itself to other areas.

To ease the discomfort of the divorce process, I got involved with someone else rather quickly — only to discover in the long run that it was impossible to avoid doing the work of learning how I had contributed to the break-down of my first marriage. I can vouch for the veracity of the old saying, "those who don't learn from history are bound to repeat it."

It has now been ten years since my divorce. I've learned that it wasn't all her fault; we both messed up our marriage. If I knew then what I know now, that marriage might have worked. Divorcing and rebuilding my life was no easier, I don't believe, than staying and rebuilding it would have been. But that's not the choice I made. I decided to divorce and build a successful new life. I did it, but it was far more difficult than I imagined.

Much of what you will learn in reading this book is what I had to learn in order to rebuild a satisfying marriage and family life. Because I had so often wanted to know the steps to success as I was struggling along, I wanted to do more than write a book that only gave information about the divorce process. I wanted to create a book that would teach others new skills that they could apply to their own life in order to ease their struggle.

Dr. Thomas Muha

EXERCISE

After reading this story, identify any similar feelings
that you might have as you face your divorce.

_____

_____

_____

_____

_____

_____

_____

_____

_____

_____

_____

_____

_____

_____

_____

_____

_____

Maureen's Story

I woke up the morning of my 27th birthday and realized I wanted to be almost anyplace else but where I was. Sure my life looked pretty good from the outside, but inside I was shutting down emotionally. We had gotten married right after finishing undergraduate school in college. Lots of our friends did too. We'd planned to go on and build our dreams together. Unfortunately, we had some very different dreams and expectations which never got fully explored in the rosy, romantic world we had constructed for ourselves in college.

Ending the marriage was painful for both of us. Interestingly enough, once I brought it up and talked about it, we were able to do it somewhat **together**! That seemed to help each of us be better able to move on in our lives. It became particularly significant for me to move on because within a year after my divorce my father died. This was followed by my mother's death 2 1/2 years later and my only brother's accidental death 3 years after that. My entire family was gone and I felt totally alone. This period was truly one with the greatest pain and the greatest growth I have had in my life so far.

I was lucky to have had a close family relationship and was able to draw on that to help me identify what types of things were important to me in creating the life I wanted. Since birthdays are always a benchmark for me I began by visualizing what it would be like when I woke up on some future birthday. Those images became important and I wrote them down and set certain goals for myself to change that image into a reality.

Believe me when I tell you I had to meet a lot of "frogs to find a prince." But in the process I was able to learn more and more about myself and the type of person with whom I wanted to share my life. With a plan and persistence I've created the life I dreamed about. I have a good marriage and a happy family with a son who's the apple of his mom's eye. Life is really looking and feeling pretty good these days!

Too often hurt and anger are so great that you feel lost and very much alone in the divorce process. It's hard to imagine next week let alone next year. Even the Lone Ranger had Tonto as a trusted friend and guide. That's where our handbook can help. Let us become your "guides" as you travel on the divorce path. The exercises we provide in the workbook draw on our own personal experiences and our professional work with thousands of people going through divorce.

Dr. Maureen Vernon

E X E R C I S E

After reading this story, identify any similar feelings
that you might have as you face your divorce.

Marie's Story

I'll never forget the day my husband told me he was divorcing me. I thought it was the worst day of my life, but I was wrong. It got worse after that when we fought over money and the kids. It got to the point that I didn't think I could take it anymore. But then we got some help about how to deal with each other as divorcing parents. It wasn't easy at first, but we began to be able to get things settled. Now we can deal with each other just like we're taking care of business on our jobs.

MARIE'S DIVORCE REACTION CHECKLIST

Divorce has a major impact on people. It can effect you in many different ways: behavioral changes, negative feelings, physical sensations, disturbing images, painful thoughts, disrupted interpersonal relations, and the development of unhealthy dependencies. This is a chance for you to assess how you are reacting to your divorce.

Everyone knows that knowledge is power. Knowing yourself gives you the power to do something about those areas of your life that are effecting you negatively. Start your journey to a successful new life as Marie did in the exercise that follows.

Marie is a 36 year old woman who had been struggling to cope with her divorce. She has two children, an 8 year old daughter, Sara, and a 6 year old son, Donny. She had been married 9 years and separated for 10 months. These are Marie's responses describing her life at that time:

✔ **BEHAVIORS:** not eating, not sleeping, not doing much of anything

✔ **FEELINGS:** sad, crying, ashamed

✔ **BODY SENSATIONS:** exhausted, nauseous

✔ **IMAGES:** living alone, unable to cope with kids

✔ **THOUGHTS:** life stinks and things are going to get even worse

✔ **RELATIONSHIPS:** men are SOBs, women friends are sympathetic

✔ **DEPENDENCIES:** wine seems to make things feel better for a time

REACTIONS TO YOUR DIVORCE

You may have only one area that's being effected, or you could have dozens of ways that your life has been impacted.

Write down today's date and then list your reactions. (Someday when you re-read this page, you'll know just how far you've come.) If you have any trouble coming up with words to describe what you've been experiencing, then simply ask yourself which area has been most effected and circle it.

DATE: _____

BEHAVIORS: _____

_____

FEELINGS: _____

_____

BODY SENSATIONS: _____

_____

IMAGES: _____

_____

THOUGHTS: _____

_____

RELATIONSHIPS: _____

_____

DEPENDENCIES: _____

_____

EARLY TRAINING FOR YOUR HOLE LIFE

If you thought programming your VCR was tough, at least they gave you a manual made specifically for your unit which you can *try* to use! Unfortunately, divorce doesn't come with an individualized manual to follow. Then how do you learn what steps to take or process to follow as you go down the divorce path?

In large part how you progress in getting out of the pits is based upon how you've seen others deal with their divorce. As you complete this section you may be amazed to discover that many of your pitfalls to progress are based upon your experiences of other people going through the stages of their divorce.

If your parents were divorced, you probably find yourself referencing how they handled it. If your experience with your parents' divorce was favorable or at least okay, chances are you will do some of the same things they did. If their divorce was a nightmare, it may still be very much a part of your life. Chances are you'll find yourself following the same road maps.

Another readily available (but not necessarily reliable) source of information and examples of how to "do divorce" comes from your friends. All you have to do is spend some time around other divorced people and you'll get an ear full of "war stories." These come complete with their list of emotional, financial and legal strategies for dealing with divorce.

While family and friends may be well-meaning and experienced, before you follow their example take a look at how well life is working for

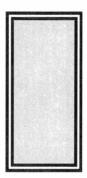

them. Is their relationship with their coparent stressful or fairly smooth? How is the child faring in the process? How well have these people been able to get out of their hole and get on with having a good life?

Remember that you know your situation better than anyone else. You can choose how you want to deal with your divorce. As you look at the models of divorce around you, select only those things that work and then continue to **learn what else will make life good for you and your child.**

EXERCISE

List the members of your own family who have been divorced
(parents, aunts/uncles, siblings).

List some things which you heard or observed them
doing as a result of their divorce.

Write down the names of any of your friends who are divorced
and list some of the things they did in the divorce process.

Review the similarities between how you have been dealing with your
divorce up to this point and how you observed others coping with their
divorces. Write out what you would like to change.

FINDING YOUR INNER STRENGTH

When we're dealing with one of life's difficulties, it can be very helpful to remember other times when we faced obstacles in our life. In particular, it can energize us if we focus on finding those times we did well at managing to overcome a problem. It brings back the feelings of confidence that we need when facing another one of life's challenges.

Darlene was fully aware of the things wrong in her life, but she didn't know what to do about it. She needed to remember the strengths and resources that she had in her life. So we asked her to think of a time when she felt proud of something she had struggled to accomplish. It could have been in school, sports, friendships, projects, work, hobbies, etc. This is how Darlene completed the exercise:

"I didn't have any money. We had just bought a new house shortly before we broke up and that had consumed all our money. I'd been at home taking care of our son, who was just about two when we separated. It wasn't the best time to leave, but I reached my limit when my husband came home drunk again. I probably should have waited to say something to him, but that still didn't give him the right to hit me. He broke three of my ribs and I think it would have been worse if our son hadn't started to scream.

Anyhow, I just felt I couldn't stay in that marriage anymore. We lost so much money having to sell the house and pay for lawyers that I had to move back in with my parents. My son and I shared a room. It was hard going through all the changes. I was afraid that my life was doomed to failure. Who would want me? I didn't have any real job skills, so I was afraid I'd never be able to support myself. I figured no man would want to take on the responsibilities of helping to raise my child.

But I got some counseling and one of the things they asked me was to remember a time when I had been successful at doing something. I thought about becoming a mother and feeling that there was so much that I didn't know about taking care of a newborn. But I had learned. I read some books, and spoke to a nurse at the pediatrician's office. I talked with my mom and some girlfriends. I turned out to be a great mother for my son.

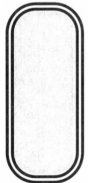

So I followed the same kind of steps to success to deal with my divorce. I read a book, got some counseling, and asked for some support from people who were close to me. I worked hard to make changes and gradually my life got better.

It even helped me get closer to my parents, and living together for awhile turned out OK. A friend told me about a nursing school nearby that had scholarships. Now I'm making good money in a job that I like. My son and I recently moved into a place I bought for us. It's in a great neighborhood and my son loves his new school."

EXERCISES

What have you done in your life that gives you the greatest sense of pride, accomplishment, fulfillment, etc.?

What were the steps that you followed in order to have achieved your goal?

(a)

(b)

(c)

(d)

(e)

Apply the steps to success that you learned from past experiences that will work for you to be able to create the new life that you have in mind for yourself:

(a)

(b)

(c)

(d)

(e)

Describe how you think you will feel after you have reached your new goals for getting out of the pits and onto the good life.

FUTURE SELF

There's an old saying in psychology, "If you don't know where you're going, you'll probably end up somewhere else." It's hard to know where you're going when all of the powerful feelings of a divorce bombard you. It's easy to get lost, stuck, or overwhelmed.

We've helped you to understand the problems and feelings associated with your divorce experience. But now what we want to do is help you to get in touch with how you want your life to be once everything's been worked out satisfactorily.

In order to be able to move on in your life, you need to have a goal in mind for how you want your life to be. Look far into your future, 5, 10, or 20 years from now when all of this has been resolved. You will have created a new life by then, the only question is how it will look and feel.

Imagine you're going to jump into a time machine. Set the dial for how many years into the future you want it to be. Let your mind actually see yourself older, wiser and happier. Imagine where you are living, and what kind of people are in your life. Think about what activities you're involved in, both personally and professionally. Be aware of all the things that you've done over the years.

To enhance your ability to create a vision, sit or lay in a comfortable position in a quiet place where you won't be disturbed. Relax your body by breathing slowly from your diaphragm. Put your hand just below the bottom of your rib cage and make it rise and fall as you breath in and out. Every time you exhale, say the word "Relax" and think about letting the tension flow out of your body. Start with the tip of your toes and relax each muscle in your body in turn until you get to the top of your head.

Playing music that you find calming can enhance the experience as well. Once you are relaxed, let your mind float forward in time. Allow the images of your future life to unfold as you come to a point in time that feels secure and satisfactory. Let yourself see what your life will be like...how you'll look . . . what you'll be doing. Imagine your life exactly as you would like it to be . . . envision what you'll be doing in your career . . . what kind of relationships you'll have . . . how you'll be enjoying your leisure time.

FUTURE SELF

What are a few of the key words that capture the essential elements of your successful future life?

_____

_____

_____

_____

_____

_____

EXERCISE:

Now draw these images in the space below. Or get a magazine and cut out pictures of things that you can use to make a collage of your new life.

REBUILD YOUR LIFE

 **R**   Recognize the importance of meeting your needs

 E   Establish a plan for creating your future

 B   Build a working relationship with the coparent

 U   Understand that win/win solutions are possible

 I   Improve your understanding of your child's needs

 L   Learn the key ingredients for helping your child with the divorce

 D   Divorce is both an ending and a beginning

CHAPTER 2

Laying the
  Groundwork for
    Coming Out
      of the "Pits"

Managing Stress and Creating

                              Balance

                              Within

                              Yourself

IF YOU DON'T KNOW WHERE YOU'RE GOING, YOU'RE THERE

I f you are going through a separation or divorce, we have good news and bad news for you. The bad news is that your life is going to change. The good news is that your life is going to change.

What makes this a bad news situation is that in the beginning of a divorce, your life is very likely going to take a change for the worse. You'll probably have only half as much money, but your bills won't be cut in half. You'll have to take care of the kids without any help at all (or at least no one to yell at because they're not helping). You'll be lonely at times, in part because you'll probably lose some of your friendships with other couples.

The stress that accompanies any major change will throw you off balance. Check out the top chart on the next page to see how stress effects anyone who is going through an upheaval in their life. But as you will also observe in the bottom chart, change and the resulting stress does *not* need to have negative long term consequences.

What's the difference? Why do some people come out of a divorce with a life that's even better, while other peoples' lives deteriorate into a living hell? There is a simple answer: CHOICES. Some folks will make choices that will create a well-balanced lifestyle that gives them what they value most in life. Other's won't.

So the good news at this point in your life is that you have a rare window of opportunity to make choices about how you want your life to be. It's much the same as if your home had burned down. You have lost a great deal, and naturally you will be having some powerful feelings about it. And lots of hassles about what it's worth with the insurance company too. But when it comes time to rebuild, you can construct a place to live that is just the way you want it to be. You'll undoubtedly keep the features you liked about the old house. But there'll be some other ways that you'll redesign your living space based on what you've learned works for you, what you've seen out in the world, and how your needs have changed as you've matured.

You have the power to make choices — to be proactive in shaping your life vs. reactive to the forces that are impacting on your life. When we react to life, we're on the defensive. We're backing away from problems rather than moving forward toward somewhere we want to be.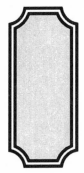

This chapter will help you develop a sense of well-being in all six areas of life: The three parts of your inner world, Body, Spirit, Mind, and the three aspects of your external world, Work, Love, and Play.

NEGATIVE STRESS PATTERN

Causes of stress:

changes	illnesses	fears	moving	work
decisions	deadlines	families	holidays	pain
emotions	commuting	money	women	men

STRESS OVERLOAD CHOICES

Short-term effects:

Body tension	Anger	Distractable	Overeating
Rapid heart beat	Anxiety	Racing mind	Drinking
High blood pressure	Depression	Poor focus	Smoking

Long-term effects:

Heart attacks	Assault & Battery	Sexual problems	Obesity
Headaches	Panic attacks	Memory problems	Alcoholism
Backaches	Suicide attempts	Sleep disorders	Diseases

WELL-BEING PATTERN

Causes of stress:

changes	illnesses	fears	moving	work
decisions	deadlines	families	holidays	pain
emotions	commuting	money	women	men

HEALTHY LIFESTYLE CHOICES

Short-term responses:

Exercise	Time management	Meditation
Relaxation	Assertiveness	Positive outlook
Nutrition	Conflict resolution	Empowerment

Long-term effects:

Fit body	Self-control	Self-esteem
Disease resistance	Satisfaction	Confidence
Proper weight	Friendships	Calmness

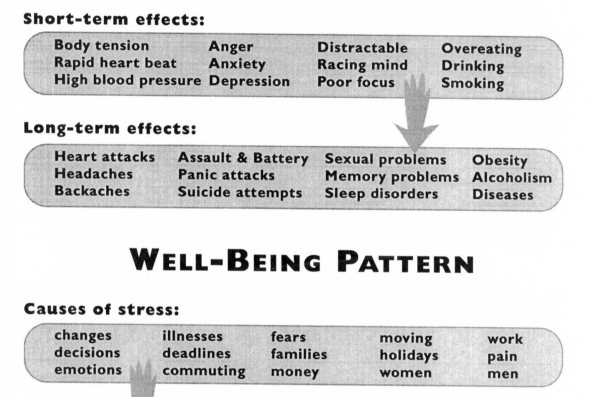

Your Body: How It Deals With Stress

The body that you are living in evolved about 30,000 years ago. The bodies of human beings have not changed very much since that time. Think about what human existence must have been like thousands of years ago — living in caves . . . nomadic clans wandering through primeval forests . . . hunting and gathering whatever food could be found.

Even 100 years ago, life was much more physically demanding. There were no cars, no electric heating or air conditioning. Many people had to hunt or grow some or all of their own food, bring in their own water, and chop wood for the fires that provided a source for heating and cooking. Anywhere you wanted to go required walking or riding a horse. For thousands of years whenever something stressful occurred, human's responded by either fighting or fleeing. So if a tiger jumped out, the choices were either using a weapon to fight the tiger off or running away to a safe place. Both choices required a person to respond physically.

But nowadays most of the time what causes us stress are "paper tigers." A great example is when you get served with court papers. And as much as we'd like to choose one of the fight/flight options, there is usually no physical response that is appropriate. But your body doesn't know that. It still fires off the adrenalin and a host of other chemicals into your blood stream, causing your muscles to tense up, your heart to start racing, and your brain to get excited. You'll begin to hear yourself say things like, "This is a pain in the neck." Or, "I'm just sick about what happened." Perhaps, "I'm breaking my back to try to take care of everything."

Because people these days don't release the tensions that build up in their body as a result of the stress in their lives, they turn instead to drugs and alcohol. Not just illegal drugs, but the whole assortment of prescription and over-the-counter remedies such as tranquilizers, antacids, aspirin, ibuprophen, etc.

Your body needs to discharge stress through some form of physical activity. Your body needs to take a walk, a run, or a bike ride. Your body would love to hit something, which in our day and age means using a tennis racquet, or golf club. Your body needs to move for 30 to 45 minutes of continuous aerobic exercise at least 3 or 4 times each week. Getting your heart rate up to 120-150 beats per minute, your body will have the chance to burn off all of the excess chemicals that build up when you're under stress.

Important Note: Consult with your physician before starting an exercise program in order to determine the safest way for you to be able to move your body without hurting it. If you have not done any exercise for awhile, start slow and build up to a more vigorous pace.

HOW WELL
Do You Take Care Of Your Body?

☐ I exercise for a minimum of 30 minutes at least 3 times every week.

☐ I give my body 7 or 8 hours of sleep at least 4 nights per week.

☐ I feed my body the right amount and types of food so that I weigh within 15 pounds of what is ideal for someone of my sex, age, and height.

☐ I take care of my body's appearance so that most days I think it looks clean, well groomed and attractive.

☐ I do something special for myself 2 or 3 times during the week such as lovemaking, massage, hot tubs or warm baths, etc.

☐ I protect my body from the poisons contained in tobacco.

☐ I respect my body by consuming no more than 2 alcoholic drinks a day.

☐ I wear a seat belt when in a car and drive defensively when behind the wheel.

☐ I put my body outdoors for the purpose of enjoying nature at least once during a week.

☐ I regularly take a breather during my day to stay more relaxed.

EXERCISE

Using those statements from above that were not checked, make some notes about how you can begin to change your lifestyle in order to be able to take better care of your body.

Why it's important for me to do this:

What I need to start doing:

Where I'll need to go:

Who I'll want to do it with me:

When I'll schedule the time to make it happen:

Your Human Spirit: The Foundation For Living Well

You have learned that your body reacts to the stress of having to contend with the myriad of problems that you face in your life You also became aware that in addition to your bodily reactions, you have the ability to make choices about how to respond to problems. But how do you decide just what to do? It's your human spirit that can tell you what will be the most valuable areas of life toward which to direct your time and energy.

Once again the concept of choice becomes important. As a child you grew up under the tremendous influence of the adults in your life. Your sense of what was important was subordinate to what those powerful adults told you. By the time you became an adult you had their scripts about what was valuable programmed into you. Maybe their scripts were accurate for those people. But it's unlikely that someone else's script from another era will be very satisfying to you today.

You need to develop your own sense of purpose in life, and then you can create the principles by which you can live your life to its fullest. After you have calmed your body, you can then open up channels of communication with the spiritual part of you. Some people

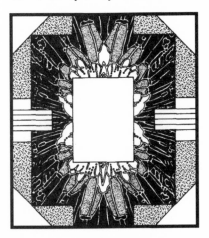

accomplish this through organized religion. But there are many methods for connecting with your spiritual self. These include avenues such as meditation, visualization, Tai Chi and self-hypnosis.

One of the simplest methods to get in touch with what is most important in your life is to find a comfortable place to do some deep breathing and relaxation. Then go forward many years in time to the very end of your life. Imagine being at the end of your life as your past flashes in front of you. What turned out to be the most significant areas to you? Note what comes to mind as first and foremost. Family? Spouse? Work? Church? Friends? Possessions? Recreation? Money? Self?

In order to go on to a satisfactory new life, you need to know what ultimately is important to you. Once you define your core values, you can make choices that will lead you to making those images real in your life. It's easy to get lost in the day to day pressures and problems of life. When your vision becomes blurred you can use your values statement as a lighthouse to orient you out of the fog and towards where it is you want to be.

1st Things 1st

Rank the following parts of your life in order of importance :

____ **Work/Career**

____ **Spouse**

____ **Money/Possessions**

____ **Friends**

____ **Health/Fitness**

____ **Parents**

____ **Relaxation**

____ **Extended Family**

____ **Personal Growth**

____ **Former Spouse**

____ **Recreation**

____ **Co-workers**

____ **Spirituality**

____ **Children**

____ **Enemies**

How Well Do You Let Your Human Spirit Take Care Of You?

It is important to know how to connect to your Human Spirit. Once you learn to relax and connect with your spiritual self, you'll be able to have a clearer image of how you can have a life based upon what is valuable to you.

Go to a peaceful place. This may be in a church, or a quiet place by the water. Or you could be in your own home where you can listen to some uplifting music or an audio tape of this exercise.

Once you've gotten comfortably settled, place your hand on your diaphragm. Let your breathing move lower in your chest so that your hand moves with each and every breath you take. Each time you inhale tense a part of your body, your facial muscles for example. Each time that you exhale, think the word **RELAX** as you let go of the tension in that part of your body. Let yourself relax completely . . . letting all of the tension drain out of your body and mind . . . closing your eyes and breathing very deeply and slowly.

After you've relaxed your face, tense and relax your jaw muscles as you breath deeply and think the word **RELAX** as you exhale. Notice how good it feels as your throat muscles let go. Continue by relaxing the back of your neck . . . relaxing your shoulders . . . relaxing your chest . . . relaxing your stomach and abdomen . . . relaxing your back . . . relaxing your arms and hands . . . relaxing your buttocks . . . relaxing your legs and feet.

As you drift down into a meditative state, you'll be able to develop the images and sensations of a light radiating from your heart . . . you'll be able to feel it's warmth . . . the glowing light will spread until it's rays are shining through your body . . . notice the color of the light . . . the light brings loving feelings with it . . . let the light illuminate your entire body and mind . . . feel your self filled with warm loving energy . . . notice that the light is also radiating it's loving energy into other areas of your life . . . basking the people there with the glow and warmth of your light . . . and you also become aware that there are other sources of light in the world that are flowing back towards you . . . through you . . . into your heart . . . connecting you to the rest of the world . . . you feel the loving energy from the world penetrating you . . . flowing through your heart and completing the connection. . . . you may become aware of a higher power from which the light of the world is streaming.

Let your mind flow to a time many years from now when your life has worked out the way you want it to be. Become aware of what is creating satisfaction in your relationships . . . in your work . . . in your recreation. Notice how your body looks and feels as it projects the calmness and confidence within your mind and spirit. See the look of pride on your face . . . feel the inner peace that comes from your being content . . . get in touch with a sense of the wisdom within you that comes from having successfully completed the journey.

IMAGES OF MY FUTURE LIFE

As soon as you open your eyes, write down everything that comes to your mind as being important to you about you and your future. Just let whatever images that come to mind flow down onto the paper.

Your Mind: Transforming Ideas Into Actions

Now that you've seen the light and have an awareness of what is most valuable about your life, you can use your conscious mind to create an action plan to make your dreams a reality. Your mind is that part of your being that gives you the self-discipline to be able to implement your ideas.

The word discipline comes from the root word disciple. A disciple is someone who believes in a specific set of values and principles, sometimes represented by a particular person or institution. Self-discipline, then, is believing in yourself and making a commitment to honor your values about what is important in the world.

Self-discipline means that you take responsibility for making choices about what you will do with your time and energy, and taking the steps that lead you in a constructive direction. Self-discipline is the opposite of playing the passive victim role and feeling angry and resentful toward others who you believe are responsible for your circumstances. Lao-Tzu, the wise founder of the Taoist philosophy, wrote:

> *He who feels punctured*
> *Must once have been a bubble.*

You have a solid set of ideas that make you extremely valuable. Whenever you doubt it, reread your values. You bring something incredibly special into the world; you're a shining star. You can make the world a better place. You have the capability of touching other peoples' lives with your loving energy.

How you spend your energy will influence how others respond. People are much like tuning forks. They will resonate to the same tune that you are sending out to them. If you transmit negative energy based on beliefs that you can't create the outcomes you want in your life, you will find that others will also respond negatively. This will appear to validate your pessimism, leaving you feeling powerless.

But if you radiate positive energy that comes from your deeply rooted values, you will find the world around you becomes harmonious with your efforts to reach your goals. You'll feel you have good luck. Remember, good luck is defined as the intersection of preparation and opportunity. You will have come into a situation prepared to work for what you believe is important for you to create. That positive energy will empower you and those around you to be able to accomplish even more than you had hoped for. After all, the whole is always greater than the sum of the parts.

How Can You Make Up Your Mind To Do What's Most Valuable?

Think of a problem that you are facing in your life at the present time and write a short summary of it:

_____
_____
_____
_____
_____
_____

Who are the people you believe are contributing to creating this problem? Describe how you think they are making your life difficult:

_____
_____
_____
_____

How have you been acting in this situation?

_____
_____
_____
_____

What is the positive outcome that would be consistent with your values in this situation?

_____
_____
_____
_____

WHEN YOU'RE STUCK IN THE PITS

Life is a trial and error experience. In the process of learning what works well in our life, we all experience many failures. Some people believe that life's best learnings come out of these failure experiences.

Thomas Edison didn't invent *the* light bulb. He invented hundreds of them, but only one of them worked! One of life's most important principles is persistence. That is what Edison was referring to when he said his success was " 1% inspiration and 99% perspiration."

To feel good about yourself you have to be able to overcome failures in your life. Your self-esteem as an adult is based on three sources: (1) your parents value of you in your childhood, (2) other people's opinion of you now, or (3) your own sense of empowerment that you know what is important and have the self-discipline to keep making the effort until you have reached your goals.

When we get stuck in the pits, it is often because we are imagining that someone else is keeping us from getting what we want. That way of thinking gives all of your power away to the other person.

You can make up your mind right now to do what you believe is important. The average American watches between 4 and 5 hours of television every day. Are you making the most of the times of your life? Your mind is capable of analyzing your schedule and figuring out when to put your priorities into place in your life. Start making responses that enable you to create the life that you have envisioned.

You can build your self-esteem by using the "Ready, Fire, Aim" approach to life. Nobody can always know what will work well. So try a variety of approaches until you hit your target. Then you'll know where to aim.

BRAINSTORMING

Write down all the ideas you can think of to try to solve a problem you are facing now. Don't evaluate what you are writing during this brainstorming process. Just put down all the possible trial and error approaches you could take.

_____
_____
_____
_____
_____
_____
_____
_____
_____
_____
_____
_____
_____
_____
_____
_____
_____
_____
_____
_____
_____
_____
_____
_____

YOUR WORK: PART 1
HOW TO HAVE ENOUGH MONEY

Your work is one of the most important parts of your life. Your economic security is based on having enough money for food, clothing and shelter for you and your children. Making more money means being able to have a more comfortable lifestyle. Having some money set aside for a rainy day increases your sense of security that you'll be able to weather life's stormy periods.

A large part of your self-image involves making a living. Working at something that makes a valuable contribution to the world is a wonderful way to feel worthwhile, but the bottom line is having some economic security.

If you are unhappy in your world of work and money, there are some questions to ask yourself in order to diagnose the problem.

1. Do you have an adequate amount of money to assure that your basic physical needs will be met?

If not, then you need to get some assistance for both your short term needs as well as your long term well-being. Contact local, state and federal agencies as well as church and charitable organizations to find out what resources they have available in the way of immediate financial aid, child support collection, job training and job opportunities.

2. Are you one of the working poor that needs to improve their lot in life?

The best way to do that is to get some additional education so that you have more to offer an employer. Explore ways of obtaining on-the-job training, continuing education classes, or home study courses.

3. Do you have a middle-class income but a wealthy person's spending habits?

Here is the lesson you need to learn in life: You can *not* buy happiness. Spending money can be like an addiction — it gives you a short term high but a long term problem. Go to someplace like a credit counseling service where they can consolidate your loans and help you stop using credit cards for a "fix." Living beyond your means only adds to the level of stress in your life.

4. Do you balance your income and spending but can't save any money?

Then you need to start paying yourself first; after all, you deserve to have some of the money that you worked so hard for. Arrange to have 5, 10, or 20% of your pay taken out of your check before you even see the money. Start talking to friends about who they trust as a financial advisor. Interview several to see who you trust. You will be amazed to discover how secure you will feel when you have some money set aside. And it's great to see an investment double in value every few years!

Making Life Work: Part 1

1. If you need help to be able to meet your basic needs:

Find these phone numbers to call for assistance with your basic needs:
- Government Agencies: Social Services (Welfare/Food Stamps), Unemployment, Medical Assistance, Child Support Enforcement/Legal Aid.
- Churches: Local Parish, Catholic Charities, Lutheran Social Services, Jewish Community Services, etc.
- Charitable Organizations: Salvation Army, Goodwill, United Way, etc.

2. If you want more education or training to get a better job:

Go ask your boss what classes he or she thinks would help you get promoted. Write down the courses that match up with what you want to do in your life:

_____

_____

_____

Follow-up by making some phone calls to explore where you can sign up for these classes: Board of Education (Continuing Education Classes), Community College, your company's human resources department, other schools in your area.

3. To be able to live within your means:

Accept that you'll never have all of the material possessions you want in life, no matter how much money you have. After you've achieved a basic level of comfort, buying material things will only give you short term satisfaction. Spend less and enjoy more! For example, agree to make gifts for family and friends and have fun doing it.

Get help with your spending habits by calling the **Consumer Credit Counseling Service at 1-800-388-CCC5** to find the office closest to you. Call them now to schedule an appointment to discuss how to get your finances under control.

Then go do something out in nature that is playful (see the Play section for more on this) in order to get some free satisfaction for yourself.

4. To have some savings:

Find the phone number of your credit union or bank. Call them now to set up an automatic deposit into your savings account every pay period. Pay yourself first. Then parcel out the rest of your paycheck to everyone else. Figure out how much you'll have at the end of the year by multiplying the amount you'll put aside each week by 52 weeks.

$_____ **per week x 52 = $** _____

YOUR WORK: PART 2
HOW TO HAVE JOB SATISFACTION

Do you hate your job most of the time? In order to enjoy your work you need to be engaged in a cooperative effort with other people to accomplish activities that you find worthwhile. If you're unhappy, three options exist for improving the situation:

1. Changing your attitude so that you're able to find more satisfaction in your work environment.
2. Changing your behavior so that the quality of your work and your working relationships improve.
3. Changing your job to work in an area of endeavor that you will find more worthwhile.

As you'll notice, the first two options involve your making adjustments. That's because you already have a lot of changes going on right now and your stress level may be contaminating your work life. Besides, the easiest place to make changes is with the one person over whom you have some control — *You.*

Perhaps your job has been so bad for so long that you are suffering from burn-out. Here are the symptoms of burn-out.

a. Chronic fatigue that not even sleep can cure

b. Irritability almost always; anger all too often

c. Chronic doubts about why you're continuing to do your job

d. Withdrawal and wanting to be left alone

e. Indiscriminate TV watching

f. Chronic dissatisfaction with your life

g. Feeling alone and out of control

h. Frequent physical illnesses and ailments

To exit the burnout expressway you'll need to change your attitude about your lifestyle. The reason people burn-out is that they become too focused on work and lose their balance because they lose touch with the other 5 areas of life: Play, Love, Body, Mind, Spirit. To change your attitude you must begin to tell yourself, "I deserve more out of life!" You'll benefit a lot from having taken the time to get in touch with your core values. An excellent book on recovering from burn-out is *It's All In Your Head* (1985, Direction Dynamics) by Bruce Baldwin.

If you are burning out on your job, stop working so much. Institute a work/play ratio of 10:1 so that for every 10 hours of work you do, you go play for 1 hour. That means you'll be needing to find 5, 6, 7, 8 hours for play time. It will be important for you to complete the section regarding **Play**.

WORK: PART 2 — EXERCISES

1. No matter what job you have, there will be good parts and bad parts.
List 3 things that are good about your present job:

    (a)

    (b)

    (c)

How can you maximize your involvement in these areas?

_____

_____

_____

_____

2. What could you do to make your job less time consuming?

_____

_____

_____

_____

3. Make a commitment to give yourself some recreation by looking at your
calendar and blocking out some play time this week. Complete this sentence:

"I deserve some pleasure in my life and I'm going to go play for
_____ hours on _____ (day)
with my friend _____."

Now you know what to do. Go for it!

LOVE:

PART 1 — FRIENDS

Dealing with your friends during your divorce will likely be a difficult task for several reasons. You are going through a time of emotional turmoil as a result of having lost your ability to trust that your primary relationship would meet your needs. With your ability to trust already on shaky ground, it's easy to find yourself approaching your friends from a position of vulnerability and uncertainty.

Your friends are going to be shaken by the news of your divorce, and their response will be directly related to their own feeling of security at the time. For example, some of your friends will undoubtedly be threatened by your divorce. They'll see you as a rival for their own boyfriend or spouse. Even if you are doing well in going on with your life, couple friends may fear that their spouses will come to see divorce as a way to resolve the problems in their marriages.

There are no good models for friends to follow about what to do with someone going through a divorce. Some people will want to take your side against your "ex" and others will judge you for "failing" in your marriage. You'll have to take the lead in guiding most people in how to deal with you during this time.

The fact of the matter is that you may only have a few intimate friendships that will survive. These relationships will be characterized by truly supportive responses inquiring about how you are doing and what you're needing. These friends will feed your self-esteem and encourage you to take care of yourself. They won't take sides in the conflicts, but help you brainstorm to find solutions to resolve your problems. Foster these types of friendships by showing your appreciation and finding opportunities to give something back by sharing some of your positive energy as well.

While a few friendships will flourish, most will flounder. Don't waste your limited emotional reserves on being resentful toward those folks who don't respond positively. Your mission is to find out which friendships will be of real value and which ones you need to let drift away. Do you want phone calls, hugs, invitations to do things together? As W.C. Fields put it,

"If you don't ask, you don't get."

Remember that friendships are like bank accounts: to keep them balanced they require that you deposit as much emotional energy as you withdraw. At the same time your friends are taking care of you, tune in to what your friends need in order to cope with whatever is going on in their lives. To have rich friendships, generate a lot of interest in what they need. Making generous deposits will create mutually supportive relationships.

PART I - EXERCISES

**List the people with whom you are friends
or who you would like to have as friends.**

_____

_____

_____

_____

_____

_____

**Identify some activities you would
enjoy doing with these people.**

_____

_____

_____

_____

_____

_____

**Think about what these friends have indicated they
are interested in doing. Write down how you
could participate with them in their activities.**

_____

_____

_____

_____

_____

LOVE:

PART 2 — FAMILY

If your family has generally been encouraging and supportive throughout your life, then you'll probably be able to count your blessings as your family comes to your assistance during this tough time.

But if your family's treatment of you has been problematic, then prepare yourself for reactions that will be consistent with the behaviors you've seen all of your life. There are strong emotions that underlie family relationships, and a stressful situation often brings out the worst in people. Your parents may see you as an extension of themselves and feel ashamed. Your siblings may be competitive and take advantage of the situation by putting you down.

The problems in your family that wounded you as a child growing up could potentially resurface during this crisis. But remember that a crisis is both a dangerous time as well as an opportunity to make changes. You are no longer a child who is defenseless against powerful adults who control your life. You have the ability to make choices now about how your life will be.

You can begin to change the way you relate to loved ones by examining your choices for dealing with your family during your divorce. Note that the emphasis here is on what *you* are going to be doing differently, not on how you wish your family would change their behavior. You only have the ability to control your own actions (and that's usually a big enough challenge in dealing with one's family!).

Here are some guidelines for dealing with family members:

1. **Maintain your privacy.** Anything you say can, and probably will, be used against you. So tell them only what you feel comfortable with having to hear about when it resurfaces.

2. **Respect their need to grieve.** Your family will also go through all the emotions associated with grieving the loss of the relationship — shock, denial, anger, depression, bargaining - until they finally accept the fact that it's over. Keeping this in mind allows you to observe their reactions from a more detached position in which you can understand what they're going through.

3. **Don't tolerate criticism of yourself.** Getting angry and defensive with your family will only create a conflict. Tell them you don't need anyone around you right now who adds any more negativity to your life. State your position in 1 or 2 sentences and do not say anything more or you'll get drawn into an unproductive argument. Simply withdraw if they persist.

4. **Don't tolerate criticism of your "ex."** Any comments that instigate or maintain your negative feelings about the coparent simply condemn you to a longer period of emotional turmoil. It also robs you of your opportunity to learn how you both contributed to the breakdown of the relationship — condemning you to a repeat of your mistakes. Finally, it destroys your child's ability to have a relationship with people they love (including you) — condemning your child to a future in which they can't trust in love.

PART 2
AN EARLY HISTORY OF THE PITS

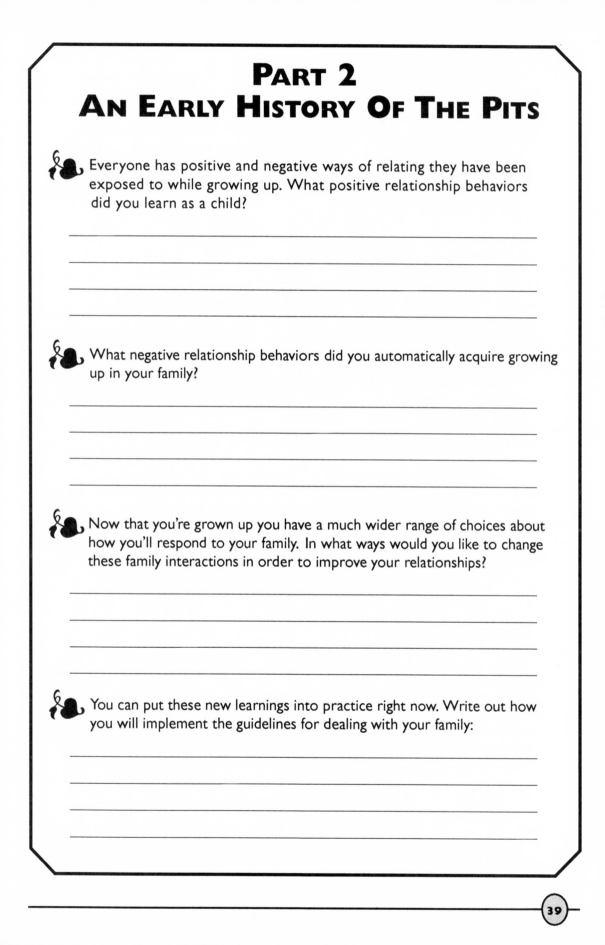

Everyone has positive and negative ways of relating they have been exposed to while growing up. What positive relationship behaviors did you learn as a child?

_____

_____

_____

_____

What negative relationship behaviors did you automatically acquire growing up in your family?

_____

_____

_____

_____

Now that you're grown up you have a much wider range of choices about how you'll respond to your family. In what ways would you like to change these family interactions in order to improve your relationships?

_____

_____

_____

_____

You can put these new learnings into practice right now. Write out how you will implement the guidelines for dealing with your family:

_____

_____

_____

_____

LOVE:

PART 3 — NEW LOVES

You've been wounded very badly going through a divorce. It may be the worst emotional pain you've ever experienced. Now is a great time for you to learn about loving relationships. Something went terribly wrong in the marriage and now is the time to learn exactly what that was. As the old saying goes, "those who do not learn from history are destined to repeat it."

You deserve to have love in your life. And you want to have a healthy love that will endure through the years. That's why now is the opportunity to learn about what went wrong, so you won't fall into the same patterns again. "Not me," you say. Well consider that the divorce rate for second marriages is even higher than for first marriages — 60%!

Since you're going to have to suffer through this divorce, you might as well get some benefit from it. Here's how. Accept that while bad things were said and done to you in your marriage, it took two people to create those circumstances. At a very minimum you chose that person to trust as the love of your life. How could you have been such a poor judge of character?

Actually, you weren't. All of the traits that you loved in the other person were all there and probably still are. But the problems of the relationship became a cancer that ate away the ability of the two of you to show those good qualities. Instead, the two of you got hooked into a pattern of negative interactions that became a vicious circle. Because you each felt hurt, you both reacted with your own negativity. Perhaps it was a cold withdrawal, or maybe it was a hot and heavy argument. Or maybe it was both of these and more.

The point is that you each contributed to the destruction of the loving feelings. It's important to remember that love is a feeling and therefore operates like all other feelings that you have. That is, your feelings are a response to what happens to you. When you are treated wonderfully, you love it. But when you are getting treated badly, you hate it.

However, the responsibility for creating the feelings in a relationship is shared by both people. When you behave lovingly toward your partner, most of the time they will respond to you positively. When you act antagonistically toward them, they will generally react with hurt and anger toward you.

That's simple enough. But also consider your reactions to your partner when they treated you badly. It takes two people to have an argument. If your partner put negative feelings into the relationship, did you put in positive feelings to provide a counterbalance? Or did you help dig the hole deeper by putting your own negative emotions into the relationship?

Remember that you contribute 50% of the feelings in the relationship, and that is a powerful influence over the other 50%. You can go on with the rest of your life committed to constructing positive connections with people. In order to have the kind of love you want, you need to know how to positively interact in your next relationship no matter how your partner may be feeling at any given time.

Part 3 — From The Pits To The Peak

Knowing how to relate with different responses in your next relationship is extremely empowering. To learn more about how to do that, write down the outrageous accusations that your "ex" has made about you:

_____

_____

_____

_____

_____

_____

Now comes the moment of truth. Well, half-truth anyway. Of course, those things were said in anger. But there was probably some grain of truth in what was said about you. Write down how a good friend would tell you the same things:

_____

_____

_____

_____

_____

With these insights, you can now develop a new script. Describe how you can relate to the people that you love in more satisfying ways from now on.

_____

_____

_____

_____

_____

Congratulations on working through this page. Developing an awareness of your old patterns of relating can be painful, but it is a tremendously productive way to bring about changes that will lead to the love you want. If you feel you need more help, contact a therapist who specializes in teaching relationship and communication skills.

$\mathcal{P}$LAY: PART 1

Buddha said, "Life is suffering." We say, "Life is a playground. Although everyone will fall and skin their knees at some time, they still enjoy recess."

Playtime is when we enjoy the fruits of our efforts. Play is the glue that holds all the other parts of life together. We know we have really let go and successfully immersed ourself in play when we say, "This is what life is all about."

Play is the time we set aside for recreation — "re-creation" of our energy reserves. This is particularly important when going through the divorce process because your personal resources become stressed to the point that it's easy to become deeply disenchanted. When you're off-balance and vulnerable, it's easy to lose perspective and make costly mistakes.

Play gives us the opportunity to have joy in our hearts, laughter in our voice and satisfaction in our soul. Having restored our balance on the playground, it's easier to remember

The Two Rules of Life:

1. Don't sweat the small stuff, and

2. It's all small stuff.

Remember when you were a young person and it was easy to slip into a playful mood. In fact it was hard to focus on getting down to business. Back then you knew just what to do to enjoy yourself. Although times have changed, you can recover that vital ability to relax and shift into the enjoyment of playful experiences once again. Give yourself permission to let the child inside of you come out to play.

Playful experiences are the highly sensory-oriented times during which you lose yourself in the pleasant process of the moment. To shift into enjoying a playful experience you must give up trying to direct the experience and simply absorb your surroundings. That means coming to your senses: seeing, hearing, feeling, smelling, tasting. By focusing on what delights your senses, you become more deeply a part of the experience.

As you become lost in the flow of being so pleasantly involved in your play, you lose your awareness of time. You respond only to the present moment with a spontaneous enhancement of doing whatever increases your emotional satisfaction. By shifting into a sensory enjoyment mode, you can make many of your experiences more playful: taking a walk at lunch, watching a sunset, smelling the crisp air on a fall day, tasting your favorite foods, hearing the sound of water trickling over the rocks, and of course, being touched and making love.

PART I — EXERCISES

Remember the playful activities you have enjoyed
that involved sensory-based experiences.
Write down some examples of pleasurable moments:

_____

_____

_____

_____

_____

_____

_____

_____

What are your 3 favorite ways to let go and enjoy the
satisfaction of coming to your senses in your play:

1.

2.

3.

PLAY:

PART 2 — BALANCING

Body, Spirit, Mind, Work, Love, and Play.

The essential ingredients of life.

Now you know what it takes to create a good life for yourself.

We're sure that you intend to give yourself what you need.

We also believe these old sayings:

> *"The road to hell is paved with good intentions."*

> **"ACTIONS SPEAK LOUDER THAN WORDS."**

> *"Just do it."*

It's the moment of truth.

Make a commitment to build a new life.

Put first things first according to your values.

Be specific.

When you're done, go celebrate the start of your new life.

You deserve to give yourself a good life.

Part 2 — Playtime Calendar

Using a ratio of 1 hour of play for every 10 hours of work, write out when you will schedule play time for yourself during the week:

Monday

Tuesday

Wednesday

Thursday

Friday

Saturday

Sunday

PLEDGE

❧ TO MYSELF ❧

Write a pledge to build a new life for yourself that will be based on your values in the six areas of life: Body, Mind, Spirit, Work, Love and Play.

I _____

Pledge to Myself to _____

_____

_____

_____

_____

_____

_____

_____

_____

CHAPTER 3

Coping With An Emotional Earthquake

Triumphing Over the Destructive Feelings of Divorce

THE STEPS TO RECOVERY

Your life has been shaken up. The very foundation of your life — your family — is crumbling into pieces. Divorce can cause a significant amount of damage in your life. The breakup of the relationship with your spouse is just the tip of the iceberg. Your dreams for the future of the family you had built together have been shattered. Now instead of trusting that your children are safe when they're with the coparent, you'll worry how well they will handle crossing the chasm caused by the divorce. Just not seeing them for days at a time when they're with the coparent is enough to send tremors running through you.

The aftershocks of divorce will effect all aspects of your life. Friends can become scared by your new status as a single person. All of your possessions will be split down the middle. Now you'll have to manage a household all by yourself, with less money and time than before. No wonder so many people suffer from a sense of insecurity about the permanence and reliability of their world. You'll probably notice some loss of self-esteem and self-confidence as you struggle with the question, "What did I do to deserve this?"

These shock waves will overshadow everything else in your life for a period of time. Even if the sun is shining brightly, some days will be dark and gloomy. When some well intentioned person tries to cheer you up with reminders of all the reasons that you have to be thankful, it won't matter. Your old life is gone. Platitudes are useless. In your heart it is pouring rain.

After all you have lost, what you need most is some glimmer of hope. You need to know you can rebuild a new life. You may be so hurt and angry that you'll have a hard time being able to imagine your life can ever be happy again. You desperately need to find the faith that you can get back onto solid ground.

Everyone has felt hopeless at times, but we've all been able to tap into the resources that we've needed. In fact, if you think about it, you can remember times in the past when you were able to draw on your own internal strength to pull you through. You may also have come to realize that you had some unexpected allies helping you along the way. Surprisingly, you may find many of the truly important pieces of your life are still there, waiting for you to pick them up and move them along with you to a new place.

The process of rebuilding will last from a few months to three years or more. The amount of time involved is directly related to the way in which you cope with your feelings in the aftermath of the divorce. There are five emotional states that you will experience - Shock/Denial, Anger, Depression, Bargaining, and Acceptance/Resolution. Achieving an emotional balance is what determines how quickly you will have the energy to build an even better life. Disasters are an inescapable part of life. They may not seem fair, but they are real. The good news is that you can survive a major earthquake and not be destroyed by it. This chapter will teach you how to use your feelings to your advantage so that you have the energy to rebuild your life.

The Shake - Up

Describe how your divorce has effected your life:

With your children -

_____

_____

_____

With your former spouse -

_____

_____

_____

With your money -

_____

_____

_____

With your home -

_____

_____

_____

With friends -

_____

_____

_____

With family -

_____

_____

_____

With your job -

_____

_____

_____

How Does It Feel To Be In The Pits?

There are five reactions to recovering from an emotional trauma. It is important to point out that everyone experiences these feelings. They are normal reactions to a very traumatic and difficult situation.

- **Shock and Denial** —when the actual physical separation occurs you may go through a period in which you feel numb and overwhelmed. As the shock leaves, the pain begins. Because the pain can be so intense at first, you may want to try to deny it by withdrawing from life.

- **Anger** — anger arises when you don't get your feelings respected or your needs met. When you are frustrated, it's easy to become angry and blame someone else for your unhappiness.

- **Bargaining** — divorce is a complex problem, but you will probably try to find a simple solution to get everything fixed right now. Because your pain is intense, you'll be tempted to strike a quick bargain in an effort to find an easy way out of having to struggle through all of the problems that you are facing.

- **Depression**— once you realize that there's no easy way out of your problems, you will either cycle back into denial or anger, or move into depression. Depression occurs when you realize you're totally powerless to change the other person and that there's no escape from your problems.

- **Acceptance/Resolution** — most people claim to have arrived at the acceptance step, only to find that feelings from the previous steps return quite easily when they're frustrated. You'll know you've arrived at acceptance when differences with your coparent arise and you're able to remain emotionally detached. Resolution occurs when you've re-established a balanced lifestyle even when a stressful situation arises.

Getting past the pain is your goal. But as the old spiritual song suggests, "It's too wide to go around, too tall to go over, too deep to go under; the only way out is through the door." You can learn to manage each of these feelings if you learn to recognize that your emotions contain positive as well as negative energy.

As you will discover in this chapter, each of these feelings will provide an opportunity for you to learn something essential about how to make your life happier. There are no mistakes in life, only lessons. These lessons keep repeating themselves until you have learned them.

Tapping into the positive energy motivates you to change some aspects of your life. As you are rebuilding, you can use your wisdom to design a more satisfying and secure lifestyle. For example, your anger will focus your attention on something dissatisfying in your life. If you allow your negative energy to flow into the situation, you'll find yourself blaming other people for the problem. But as you come to recognize that your anger is based on a need being frustrated, you'll start to think about what *you* can do to get what you want.

Earthquake Reaction Checklist

I f you check any of the boxes below, it will be an indication that you need to address some of the feelings you still have about your divorce in the pages that follow. If you don't do this work now, the feelings will just keep reoccurring as an indication that you have unresolved issues.

SHOCK/DENIAL

- ☐ I can't believe this is happening to me.
- ☐ Our problems aren't serious enough to lead to divorce.
- ☐ I'm feeling weak and drained of energy.
- ☐ I'm having trouble with my eating and sleeping patterns.
- ☐ I keep expecting my spouse to come back.
- ☐ I'm so overwhelmed, I'm unable to perform routine tasks.

ANGER

- ☐ This divorce isn't my fault.
- ☐ There's nothing good to say about my ex.
- ☐ This shouldn't have happened to me.
- ☐ All of my problems have been caused by my ex.
- ☐ My ex is doing this to me because she/he is a sick person.
- ☐ I hate my ex for hurting me and the children.

BARGAINING

- ☐ I'll try almost anything to make the pain go away.
- ☐ I find myself drinking alcohol more than I used to.
- ☐ I've started taking drugs (prescription or otherwise).
- ☐ I'm in another relationship within a few months of my separation.
- ☐ I'll agree to almost any settlement just to get the papers signed.
- ☐ I'd be willing to try a reconciliation right now.

DEPRESSION

- ☐ I'll never be loved again.
- ☐ I'm powerless to change my situation.
- ☐ I haven't had any fun for weeks now. I'll never be happy!
- ☐ At times I think I'd be better off dead.
- ☐ I can't trust anyone anymore.
- ☐ I've stopped taking very good care of myself.

ACCEPTANCE/RESOLUTION

- ☐ I can talk to my ex without getting hooked into negative reactions.
- ☐ I recognize that I contributed to the problems in my marriage.
- ☐ I have some ideas about what would make my life happier.
- ☐ I actually do some good things for myself everyday.
- ☐ I can accept my children loving both of us.
- ☐ I feel that I have a balanced lifestyle in terms of my body, spirit, mind, work, love and play.

THIS CAN'T BE HAPPENING: SHOCK/DENIAL

The first step in dealing with your divorce is to overcome your feelings of shock and denial. You may have been trying to ignore the signals which were shouting out the message that your marriage was terminally ill. But now the numbing reality is here. Either you or your spouse has moved out and you may be feeling a sudden sense of abandonment. The shock of separation creates feelings that range from apprehensiveness to anxiety to outright panic. Many people feel shaken to the core, both physically and emotionally. They find themselves having problems being able to concentrate.

All of these reactions are normal and you need to keep reminding yourself of that. Using denial protects us from our pain. And the pain involved in a divorce is incredible. Your sleep patterns may be totally disrupted, and you may find yourself going through periods where you sleep too much. Then there will be times when you can't sleep at all. You may find you frequently have a dry mouth, and that your body in general is afflicted by aches and pains. Your mind feels like it's "out of it." You'll have thoughts revolving around your ex. You may be unable to function in the normal routines of life.

Denial is a frequently utilized first line of defense. By pretending not to know something, you hope that it will go away and your pain will stop. The old adage "What you don't know can't hurt you" usually backfires and causes you to be immobilized and unprepared to deal with the events that are happening in your life. The temptation to retreat into denial as a refuge from your pain is like denying that you have bills to pay. You can happily go along with your life until your car gets repossessed and the landlord tells you to move.

The feeling that often accompanies the denial stage is fear. What will my family and friends think of me? What will happen to my children? So many of these questions can surface that you don't want to have to face the reality of it all. You just can't imagine that you'll

be able to cope with all the changes that are occurring in your life. So you avoid it for awhile, hoping against hope that a miracle will occur and make it all better. But when you do nothing, that's just how much progress you make towards rebuilding your life.

Initially divorce seems like a bad dream and you keep thinking, "This can't be happening." So you may withdraw and take a passive role in which you're confused and incapacitated. Or you take an active role and imagine that you can jump straight to acceptance and resolution and move on with your life without any pain at all. Neither way out will work. So find a friend and face your pain. Tell yourself, "This pain is one of the steps on my journey to recovery. I will not always feel like this."

In order to face your pain you will benefit from reaching out to others for help. Find a counselor, a minister, a support group, family members and some friends you can turn to. Write their phone numbers on a piece of paper and call them when you need help to get through the hurt that you are experiencing.

The SHOCKING Truth About Fear

What's most frightening to you about your divorce?

_____

_____

_____

_____

Remember how you were able to overcome a fear you had to face at some time in your past. Write down what worked for you to be able to do that:

_____

_____

_____

_____

Describe how you felt once you had conquered your fear:

_____

_____

_____

_____

Memorize that feeling so you can breathe and relax and conjure up that strength whenever you need it. Describe how you'll do that the next time your fears surface and you want to give yourself a good feeling.

_____

_____

_____

_____

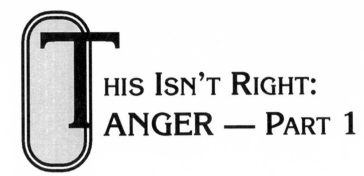

THIS ISN'T RIGHT: ANGER — PART 1

nger is an emotion in which you can become trapped. You life is in shambles and you want to know who is at fault for the collapse. Anger occurs when you blame someone else for what has happened to you. "But they did me wrong," you say. While that is probably true, blaming doesn't help you to make things any better.

Anger only increases your feelings of being powerless. Blaming somebody else for your problems puts the focus on what they are doing to contribute to making your life miserable. Since you don't have any control over them, you are trapped into becoming more and more enraged because they won't change and start doing what you want them to do. In fact, they may seem to get some satisfaction out of seeing you suffer.

But you can take that power away from them by understanding how to change your blind rage reaction into a reasoned response. Managing your feelings is something that you learned to do, and those skills can be improved upon. You first learned to deal with anger during your childhood and adolescence. That was a time when you had much less power than your parents. There were often situations in your youth in which your needs were frustrated and there was nothing you could do about it except be angry.

Similar situations arose in your marriage when you, once again, found yourself depending on a loved one to meet your needs. It's extremely painful when a loved one lets you down. You often react like you did when you were a child — you become increasingly enraged when you don't get what you want from someone you think should be treating you well.

The purpose of becoming angry is to try to get control over a situation that is unacceptable to you. Does becoming angry accomplish that outcome or does it only cause the problem to escalate further out of control? In order to address a problem situation with another person, you need to start with managing the 50% of the relationship that is under your control — *yourself.*

When you are in a situation that you perceive as a threat to you, your body will react with a fight or flight response. You will get a surge of adrenalin, your breathing and heart rate will become faster, and your mind will race as it frantically prepares to defend you. You become flooded with feelings as you prepare to fight your attacker or to run away from him. These are automatic reactions that humans acquired thousands of years ago when threats were always physical and we needed our body to fire up in order to fend off the attack.

These same reactions occur within your body even though nowadays many of the threats that you face are directed toward your psychological well-being. For example, "I'm going to take you to court." In order to begin to deal with a threat, you will first need to calm your body and your mind. Thinking and feeling are opposites. When flooded with feelings, you can't think clearly. Calming yourself allows you to use your mind so you can use the skills that will have the best chance of resolving the problem in a non-confrontational manner.

How I React When I'm ANGRY

When you were growing up, how did the people in your family handle their anger? Describe the way anger was shown:

FATHER:

_____

_____

_____

MOTHER:

_____

_____

_____

YOURSELF:

_____

_____

_____

_____

When you get angry now, how does your body react as you become flooded with feelings?

_____

_____

_____

In a situation that angers you, what are the thoughts that race through your mind at that time?

_____

_____

_____

By now you are probably noticing some similarities as you realize that you are playing out old patterns that you learned as a child. This recognition is an important first step toward making a conscious effort to learn to use more effective techniques to cope with stress and frustration. To have the faith in yourself that you can learn to do this, let your spirit make this pledge:

"I WANT TO LEARN TO CONTROL MY ANGER BECAUSE I WANT TO HAVE THE POWER TO BE HAPPY IN MY RELATIONSHIPS."

FIGHTING, FLEEING OR FIXING IT: ANGER — PART 2

When we become angry we have four options for how to handle our feelings. The first choice is to let go of our emotional controls and become openly aggressive. It's important to note that verbal or physical aggression is the result of making a choice about how to deal with an unsatisfactory situation.

Many people want to say, "You made me mad." **WRONG**. Nobody has the power to control your feelings except for you. Venting angry feelings aggressively is a choice that one person makes in an attempt to force another individual to comply with their demands. This destroys relationships.

The second choice for handling anger is to suppress it. Some people think it's bad to express any angry feelings. So they stuff their anger down into the dark recesses of their mind where it festers until it can find some indirect means of expression. For example, a wife gets mad at her husband, but says nothing. Later she develops a headache, becomes moody and retires to bed early.

The third choice people make in dealing with anger is to become passive-aggressive. These individuals recognize that open aggression will only lead to ugly confrontations. They also don't feel they can ignore a situation in which they're not getting what they want. So they pout and use the "silent treatment." They become only half-heartedly involved in the relationship, and are often deliberately obstinate. They want to have control over the situation with the least amount of vulnerability. But this choice only intensifies the problem.

The fourth choice for dealing with anger is to find a healthy way to direct your energy toward improving the situation. Using stress management techniques allow you to discharge the negative energy associated with anger. Releasing the tension in your body takes at least 30 minutes. Exercising helps to burn off the adrenalin and practicing some form of meditation can calm your mind.

Your anger is fed by your dwelling on thoughts that the other person involved in the problem is wrong, that they have intentionally hurt you, and that they deserve to be pun-

ished. These thoughts will eventually lead you to making a destructive response that will only add fuel to the fire. Instead, you can change your thinking and become focused on fixing the problem.

For example, the coparent has brought the kids back late from visitation several times. At first you think, "He's so irresponsible! He doesn't care that his own kids are getting to bed too late and are tired the next day in school." But you give yourself 30 minutes to relax and then ask yourself how you'd like things to be. You start thinking about needing his cooperation in order to get him to stick to the schedule. You begin brainstorming possibilities of what you can do to elicit increased cooperation: Show him a video of having to drag the kids out of bed the next morning, get reports from the teachers about the kids performance in school the day after visitation, etc. You'll find yourself beginning to have more positive, optimistic feelings.

Exploding The Myths About Anger

In your marriage, how did your spouse handle anger?

_____

_____

_____

How did you handle your anger during the marriage?

_____

_____

_____

How are you and your former spouse handling your anger during the divorce?

_____

_____

_____

What can you do to allow your body to relax before you respond?

_____

_____

_____

Reread the example of kids coming home late from visitation. What thoughts do you have about what would work to redirect your mind away from getting revenge and into calmly finding a cooperative way to solve the problem?

_____

_____

_____

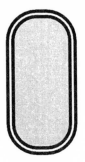

I'm Not Taking It Anymore: Anger — Part 3

Anger does not work to make your life better. In fact, being angry is a powerless position that has not worked for you at any stage in your life. Your divorce provides you with an excellent opportunity to learn how to let go of angry feelings so you can learn to be effective in coping with life's problems. When you feel the old anger pattern beginning, you can choose how you will react.

Communicating Anger Constructively. Changing your thoughts will give you the right attitude. Changing your words will give you the results you want! Your goal is to be able to say something that communicates your point of view *in a way that does not create defensiveness.* You want the other person to be receptive to your statement. To accomplish this, there are some specific guidelines that must be followed:

1. Ask for 5 minutes of uninterrupted time to discuss just one topic.

2. Identify what you are feeling **without blaming the other person.** To do that, do not talk about the other person when you discuss the problem. Instead of using the word "you," make "I" statements. Describe your own feelings that arose in the situation without saying anything about the other person. Simply say, "When _____ happens, I feel_____."

Example: *"When the kids come home late from visitation, I feel angry and worried."*

3. Explain your feelings briefly without any criticism or contempt. Simply describe the reasons for your frustrations in terms of the negative consequences that it is creating.

Example: *"They have very little time to finish their homework. As a result, they're often late getting to bed and then they're tired the next day. I'm angry about having to deal with cranky kids on a regular basis, and I'm worried about how it's effecting them in school."*

4. Make every effort to gain the coparent's cooperation by appealing to his or her sense of concern for the well-being of the children. Tell them what you want is to work out a mutually satisfying solution to the issue that has arisen.

Example: *"I know that you want the kids to do well in school. What I'd like to do is find a solution that works for both of us so that we can be sure that the children are getting what they need to get their homework done and get their rest."*

5. Remember that the coparent is accustomed to arguing, so they may try to hook you into a fight by attacking you. If you become angry, take some slow, deep breaths. Tell yourself you have the power to recognize when someone is using a tactic designed to knock you off balance. Then use the "broken record" technique of simply restating your message until the coparent finally comes to understand that you are going to persist in addressing the issue in a constructive way.

Expressing Anger Constructively

What is something that you are angry about regarding your divorce?

_____
_____
_____

Write out a rough draft of how you address this issue following the 5 guidelines for communicating your anger constructively.

_____
_____
_____
_____
_____
_____
_____
_____
_____

Now rewrite that statement taking out any criticisms, judgements, accusations or other "blame game" messages that refer to the coparent's motivation, attitude or character.

_____
_____
_____
_____
_____

I JUST WANT TO GET IT OVER WITH: BARGAINING

At some point you realize that no matter how hard you try to deny what's going on or how angry you get about it, you still have to deal with the difficulties of your divorce.

You can get trapped into wanting to make it all better right now. Just stop the pain somehow. You search for some simple solution to all of the problems brought on by the divorce: drugs, alcohol, affairs, workaholism, reconciliation fantasies, food, shopping, etc. The trouble with simple solutions, of course, is that they simply are futile attempts to find an easy way out of a very complicated situation. It's easy to get addicted to something that makes you feel better, even if it's a short-lived "fix."

To successfully conclude your divorce, you will need to have a satisfactory negotiation process. Many marriages have problems with a power imbalance between the partners. One person plays a dominant role while the other is in the passive/submissive role. The same imbalance that existed during the marriage can continue in the bargaining process.

When there is inequality in a relationship one partner tries to force the other to operate according to what they believe is right, needed, and should happen. The passive partner initially buys into this scheme because they get the love and affection, as well as the direction and protection that they were seeking. However, as the dominant partner builds their self-image by being seen as all-powerful, they do so at the expense of their partner's sense of self-worth.

By giving away their own power to the dominant partner in exchange for love, the passive person must deny their own feelings, needs, and values as they defer to their partner. Typically the dominant partner reinforces this process by treating with contempt any efforts the passive person makes to share their point of view. Eventually the passive person lapses into depression, or they rebel and begin to seek power outside of the marriage: working, drinking, or having an affair. Frequently they become passive/aggressive in the marriage as they become increasingly critical of the dominant partner's decisions. This infuriates the dominant partner who reacts with intensified aggression, defending their controlling behavior by rationalilzing they were only doing what was "right" to take care of the family.

Power struggles ultimately destroy marriages, and they produce very ugly divorces as well. The break up of your marriage will provide you with the opportunity to learn how you contribute to the power struggle. If you think there is a winner and a loser, a villain and a victim, then you will continue a style of bargaining in your divorce that is designed to right the wrongs and punish your "ex."

But no one wins in a power struggle. That way of relating helped to destroy your marriage and it will continue to damage your life unless you learn to recognize your role in creating the conflict. You can learn to negotiate a mutually acceptable divorce settlement. Those skills will help create more equality and security in your next relationship.

Identifying Your Power Position

How to tell if you were the dominant partner:

- ☐ You don't think the marriage was all that bad.
- ☐ You deny the accusations that you were "controlling."
- ☐ To this day you can see the vision of how the marriage could have worked out.
- ☐ You know exactly what your "ex" should have done differently in order to have saved the marriage.
- ☐ You're angry that your partner changed and feel betrayed by them.
- ☐ You can't believe they left you and think they must be crazy.

How to tell if you were the passive partner:

- ☐ You began to enjoy doing new things and became involved in new activities with a variety of people other than your mate.
- ☐ You pointed out repeatedly just exactly how your spouse was failing to make the marriage a happy one.
- ☐ You think your spouse should have known what you wanted and that you were so unhappy because you weren't getting it.
- ☐ When you were with your spouse you felt like a different person who was unable to be yourself.
- ☐ Before the separation you had begun to deceive your spouse and had gone behind their back to get what you wanted.
- ☐ You initiated the divorce because you had lapsed into total despair about being able to get what you wanted.

IF YOU WERE THE DOMINANT PARTNER: You had a good relationship once upon a time and you were angry when it changed. But the way to have some control in a relationship is to share the power with the other person by learning how to arrive at mutually agreeable decisions. What will you do differently in the future?

_____

_____

_____

IF YOU WERE THE PASSIVE PARTNER: Hopefully you have come to recognize that your inability to be direct in asserting your needs was a major factor in not getting them met. The same will be true during and after your divorce. How will you learn to say what you want and be strong in negotiating for it?

_____

_____

_____

EPRESSION: PART 1

What happens when you conclude that nothing you can do will change your marriage? You leave with the determination that you can have a better life. But your divorce has been pretty much of a failure experience as well. Suddenly you feel insecure.

A frightening feeling comes over you when you realize that you are on your own trying to build a new life. Your self-esteem has suffered during the battles of the break-up of your marriage. And now you have all kinds of new responsibilities that feel overwhelming. You aren't sure you're up to it.

There are times that you conclude there is nothing you can do to make things work out the way you want them to. You may feel like giving up on everything, including life. Terrifying thoughts can circulate through your mind, for example - "I'll never have love. I'll never be happy again".

Depression is a common feeling to have during a divorce. Your feelings of depression may fall in a range from mild to severe. If you are seriously contemplating suicide or homicide, then you need to talk to a counselor NOW. These thoughts arise when you think there is no other way out of your pain. You are stuck in the pits, but a mental health professional can help you find solutions to get you into a better place.

Other ways of becoming stuck in depression occur if you withdraw from life. Eating and sleeping become serious problems. You are all alone with your negative thoughts about being hopeless, worthless, guilty, and unlovable. Nothing gives you pleasure anymore. You're resigned to giving in to the demons of depression and suffering a bleak existence.

If you stay stuck in that severe level of depression for more than two weeks, then you need the help of a psychotherapist. You will learn that there are ways of beating depression. These include medications, exercise, and help to change your ways of thinking to become more positive in your approach to life. Your mind is like a computer when it comes to figuring out how to solve problems. The rule "garbage in, garbage out" applies to the way your mind thinks about problems. If you program yourself with thoughts about how awful things are, then you'll stay stuck because you won't see any positive actions that you could take.

Depression in smaller doses helps you to look at what you did to contribute to the problems. Of course that feels terrible. But when you are able to apply these learnings to make changes in your priorities and actions, then you'll begin to feel better. You are not going to want to suffer through another divorce. So learn everything you can about how to give yourself a good life.

When you get angry, you are blaming someone else for your troubles. When you get depressed you are blaming yourself. Neither of these feelings will help you to do anything to actually make your life any better. The ingredients of a happy life are skills that you can learn. When you think of something you did that you regret, ask yourself what you will learn to do differently in the future.

Identifying Depression

Depression falls on a continuum from mild to severe. The depth of your depression will be determined by two factors: your thoughts and your behaviors. Your total score on this questionnaire is less important than if you feel your depression is more than you want to deal with on your own. If so, find a good therapist who can help you to get out of the pits and on to a good life.

Circle any that apply to you: 1 = mild   2 = moderate   3 = severe

1	2	3	I'm afraid people are looking down on me now.
1	2	3	I won't be accepted by my friends anymore.
1	2	3	I'm more comfortable just staying at home.
1	2	3	I have to put on an act around other people.
1	2	3	I spend a lot of my time working.
1	2	3	It looks like my life will be lonely.
1	2	3	I have a hard time talking to other people.
1	2	3	It's more important that I just take care of others.
1	2	3	I'll never have a love life again.
1	2	3	I watch TV indiscriminately.
1	2	3	I was a lousy spouse.
1	2	3	My spouse was even worse.
1	2	3	They never thought of my needs.
1	2	3	They treated me unfairly.
1	2	3	They ruined our marriage.
1	2	3	But I'll be blamed for the break-up.
1	2	3	If we had just tried a little harder.
1	2	3	I don't know if I'll survive this.
1	2	3	I'm feeling ill quite often.
1	2	3	My weight has changed significantly.
1	2	3	I often think about ending it all.

DEPRESSION: PART 2

You have probably had some times during the divorce when you were in the pits of depression to one degree or another. Depression can signal a turning point in your life because it is an opportunity to discover ways of thinking and behaving that can actually help you turn your life around.

When you hit bottom, you have three choices. First, you can try to escape the pain by going back to previous reactions such as denial or anger. Second, you can make the "no choice" choice. That is, you can choose to do nothing and become chronically depressed. Or third, you can choose to take responsibility for your thoughts and behaviors and change them.

Changing your ways of thinking and behaving is the break-through technology of psychology. Choosing what you think will change how you behave. So the next time you are thinking about how awful your life is you can make a choice to give equal time to thinking about your values and needs.

People distort their thinking in many ways that make life seem harder than it is. One type of distorted thinking is to imagine the worst case scenario, and then to feel as if that is definitely what will happen. This way of thinking actually contributes to creating negative outcomes by passively accepting what is erroneously assumed to be inevitable. One becomes paralyzed instead of mobilizing resources to find alternatives.

Another type of distortion is all or nothing thinking. This often happens when we use words such as "always" or "never" to describe someone's behavior. Nothing about people is absolutely true all of the time. When we start to think so, we put ourselves into conflict with that person who will have a long list of times to tell you about when it was not true.

Other words that signal trouble are "should" and "must." When you use these words with someone else you are passing judgement about what the right thing is for them to do. Since no one likes to be told what to do, this way of thinking will lead you to saying something that will only bring about conflict. When you apply these words to yourself, you create unrealistic expectations which often lead to disappointment, frustration, or further depression.

There are other ways of thinking that produce positive results and good feelings. For example, thinking about what you want, what others may be needing, and how everybody can get most of what they want, generates much more positive energy for you and your relationships.

You can decide what you think would work out well in your life and you can choose to take an action step toward realizing that outcome. And when you do, you'll feel terrific. You will have empowered yourself because you will have begun to change your life toward the direction you want it to go.

You will no longer be controlled by other people or by your own negativity. By recognizing there are things that you need to work on in your life, you have come face to face with how you have given away your power through much of your life. By facing the demons of your depression, you'll discover you have the ability to change your thinking to focus on solutions about what will make you happy. And you will unleash the power to make choices to adopt behaviors that will lead you step-by-step toward that lifestyle.

Overcoming Depression

Write down the thoughts you're having about what the coparent should or should not be doing in dealing with the problems of your marriage and divorce.

_____

_____

_____

What is the worst thing that can happen as a result of these problems?

_____

_____

_____

What is something that the coparent "always" does or "never" does that really bothers you?

_____

_____

_____

Extract the learnings that these lessons in distorted thinking can provide. When you find yourself in a similar situation, what new thoughts will be important to have in mind about creating positive outcomes in your life?

_____

_____

_____

Based on these positive thoughts, what would you do to contribute to creating a positive outcome?

_____

_____

_____

Acceptance is Different Than Agreement

Acceptance occurs when you've experienced a sense of loss regarding your marriage and you no longer feel caught in the pits of anger and depression. You are able to reflect on the good and bad parts of the relationship as learnings in your life. You can now move on to accept the ending of the marriage with some sense of peace and dignity.

The block to arriving at acceptance will be an inability to forgive your spouse. "But", you say, "my ex doesn't deserve to be forgiven after all they've done to me!" While forgiveness may benefit your spouse, it is primarily going to help you because it is going to free you of all of the negative emotions that have been plaguing you about the divorce. If you don't forgive them, you condemn yourself to staying stuck in the pits forever.

Most people imagine that they've accepted their divorce long before they actually have. The true test is how you react when problems arise. If you have learned that problems are just a part of life (and divorce), then you don't start blaming yourself or someone else when they arise. Instead, you shift into a problem solving mode and start searching for solutions.

To be able to accomplish this shift, you have to be able to let go of the negative emotions. You need to know how to cope with your feelings of anger and/or depression. You see yourself as having equal power with the other people involved in the situation. You are aware that your choices will profoundly effect the course of your life. You know where you want to be. You recognize that you are capable of thinking through the current problem in order to be able to generate mutually satisfying solutions.

How do you "let go" of the negative emotions toward someone who has hurt you? By telling yourself that you are not going to let the hurt continue by carrying it around within you. That means whenever you start blaming or feeling guilty, you tell yourself that mistakes are part of being human. You tell yourself that you forgive failings, yours and others. You accept the fact that life is a trial and error experience, with mistakes merely being a step in the process of learning to manage life more successfully.

As you stop beating yourself and others up for how you've been hurt, you see yourself on the pathway of life with all it's ups and downs. You accept that people learn by taking two or three steps forward and then one backward. You know what you want to create in your life and you pursue those activities that help you to move toward where you want to be.

Your past has primarily been put to rest. Occasionally you remember and have regrets, but you're able to balance your emotional state by being aware of your accomplishments. The present moment becomes what is most important to you because that is the only point at which you can make choices. Making choices gives you the power to try out different solutions as your search for what will bring you happiness in life. Choices are the chisel that you use to sculpt your life.

PUTTING FORGIVENESS INTO PRACTICE

 Write down how you've been hurt and at the end add, "and I forgive you."

_____

_____

_____

_____

 To be able to stay in touch with the good feelings that acceptance can bring, take a few minutes to do the following imagery exercise:

Imagine that you can float above your body and look at yourself from a different 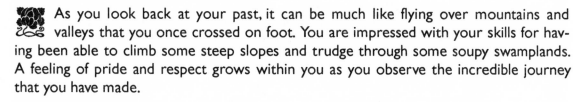 perspective. Looking over your life, you can see the flow of time moving from what is behind you to what lies ahead in your future.

As you look back at your past, it can be much like flying over mountains and valleys that you once crossed on foot. You are impressed with your skills for having been able to climb some steep slopes and trudge through some soupy swamplands. A feeling of pride and respect grows within you as you observe the incredible journey that you have made.

You begin to drift forward into the future, seeing yourself continuing the adventure. Pay close attention to how you use your learnings of the past to make good choices about how to progress along life's pathways. Feel your confidence building as you overcome obstacles along the way.

See yourself creating a lifestyle that is based upon the values you have had in mind regarding your Body ... Mind ... Spirit ... Work ... Love ... Play.

As you feel a sense of acceptance that your life will turn out well, notice there will be something about your vision of the future that symbolizes your happiness.

 Write that symbol down as a resource that you can always turn to when you need to encourage yourself.

_____

_____

_____

_____

Acceptance: Drawing From Your Past To Design Your Future

As you progress through the emotional reactions of your divorce, you'll slowly begin to work out all the details of your life. By this stage of your life you have faced other problems that you were able to solve. You have the inner resources to step up to this challenge. By identifying that part of you that has been successful in solving problems in the past, you will find the strength and courage to do that now.

In this chapter you have worked through the feelings that often block people from going on with their lives. There is an old story about an ancient tribe who would force their members to walk through THE ROOM OF A THOUSAND DEMONS. It was explained to them that the demons' only power was to know your worst fears and assume that shape. So that if you were afraid of snakes, you would be faced with the illusion of having to walk through a room filled with a thousand snakes. But in spite of the fact that people were told that these forms were merely illusions, many people panicked and self-destructed. So a very simple rule was developed to help people move through the room of a thousand demons: No matter what, keep your feet moving.

Go back to happier times in your life when you felt like your "normal self." Remember when you were feeling good about how you were coping with your life. How old were you at that time? Where in your body did you feel the good feelings of being able to cope? Think about the ways you were successful in coping with your stress and tension when you were your "normal self. Picture yourself in your mind as you see yourself feeling proud and confident. Hear the positive statements you are saying to yourself about how well you were able to manage your life at that time. Always remember that you can draw upon this healthy and well-functioning "normal self." Whenever you need to have this part advise you, you can see, hear and feel these images you just experienced.

USING YOUR INNER RESOURCES

Think of a minor problem you are experiencing now. You've solved minor problems before, and of course, you will again. Using the minor problem that came to mind, fill in the blanks in these sentences:

I have successfully coped with problems in the past, such as the time I resolved the situation involving ...

_____

_____

_____

_____

Using the strategies that were successful in the past, what would work well to solve the minor problem you're experiencing now?

_____

_____

_____

_____

Continue to use this strategy for giving your "self" positive feelings as you think about how you can deal with the things that are distressing to you now.

A problem that I was proud of having solved in the past was ...

_____

_____

_____

_____

By using the same strategy, I will successfully resolve some of my present problems by ...

_____

_____

_____

_____

ADDITIONAL RESOURCES:

Helpful Books For Divorcing Parents

Families Apart: Ten Keys to Successful Co-Parenting, Melinda Blau (New York: G. P. Putnam's Sons, 1994).

Getting Apart Together, Martin Kranitz (San Luis Obispo, CA: Impact Publications, 1987).

Helping Children Cope with Separation and Loss, Claudia Jewett (Harvard Common, 1982).

Helping Children of Divorce, Susan A. Diamond (New York: Schocken, 1985).

How It Feels When Parents Divorce, Jill Krementz (New York: Knopf, 1988).

How to Forgive Your Ex-husband and Get On with Your Life, Marcia Hootman and Patt Perkins (New York: Warner, 1985).

In Praise of Single Parents, Shoshana Alexander (New York: Houghton Mifflin, 1994).

Long Distance Parenting, Miriam Cohen (New York: Cignet Books, 1989).

Mom's House, Dad's House: Making Shared Custody Work, Isolina Ricce (New York: Collier Books, 1980).

My Kids Don't Live with Me Anymore, Doreen Virtue (San Francisco, CA: Hazelden, 1988).

The Parents Book About Divorce, Richard A. Gardner (New York: Bantam, 1977).

Resolving Conflicts: With Others and Within Yourself, Gini Graham Scott (Oakland, CA: New Harbinger Publications, 1990).

Second Chances, Judith S. Wallerstein and Sandra Blakeslee (New York: Ticknor & Fields, 1989).

Sharing Parenthood after Divorce: An Enlightened Child Custody Guide for Mothers, Fathers, and Kids, Ciji Ware (New York: Viking, 1982).

Solo Parenting: Your Essential Guide, Kathleen McCoy (New American Library, 1987).

Surviving the Breakup: How Children and Parents Cope with Divorce, Judith S. Wallerstein and Joan Berlin Kelly (New York: Basic, 1980).

CHAPTER 4

Stop Mud Slinging And Find Common Ground

Resolving Conflicts with the Other Parent

ONFLICT RESOLUTION DURING THE DIVORCE PROCESS

Divorcing can be much like going to war. Each side blames the other for starting the conflict. As hostilities escalate, the opposing sides find more and more reasons to continue battling. Both sides complain bitterly about the attrocities committed by the other. No communication is possible as each party focuses all of their energy into attacking the opposing position while defending their own.

War is hell and divorce battles are no exception. If issues are not resolved by agreement, then you will have to go to court and let a judge decide. Seldom are there ever winners, because the losers will continue to fight.

This is a very expensive method of resolving conflicts; child custody battles costing $5,000-$10,000 or more are a prime example. We've known people who spent their last penny on lawyers rather than arrive at an agreement that would have preserved their capital and their sanity. It is cheaper and more effective to reason and compromise early in the process than it is to have the courts force a decision upon you.

Conflicts between divorcing couples are inevitable. Many decisions need to be made during a time of emotional turmoil by two people who couldn't resolve their problems satisfactorily when they were still living together. However, it is highly improbable that you will engage in an argument over your differences and have the other side suddenly surrender. Attacking the other person or defending your position will only polarize the situation even further.

Divorce does not have to be this way. Arguments cannot occur without two willing participants. That's right. If you are not willing to engage in the battle, then the fighting will stop. Think about it. Can an argument continue if only one person is participating? This does not mean that the coparent won't act badly at times. It means that **you** have the power to unilaterally decide what your response will be. Your response will determine whether or not a battle will rage.

To accomplish this feat, simply remember the rule "Don't fight, don't give in." Most people who hear this for the first time are perplexed. They ask, "What else can I do?" The answer involves learning communication skills that are necessary in any type of successful relationship: (1) communicating your position confidently, (2) listening to the other person's point of view, and (3) developing an understanding of what each side needs for a mutually satisfying resolution of the conflict.

If you enter into negotiations over issues involving the children or property with the attitude that you can eventually arrive at an agreement that is mutually acceptable, then you'll be able to focus on following the steps that will lead to a resolution. Many people (some just as skeptical as you may be) have learned how to do this. You can too.

CHECKLIST
OF POTENTIAL CONFLICTS

❏ Custody

❏ Visitation

❏ Holidays

❏ Child Support

❏ Birthdays

❏ School Vacations

❏ Pick-Up/Drop Off

❏ Education

❏ Discipline

❏ Grandparents

❏ Health Insurance

❏ Life Insurance

❏ Child Abuse

❏ Badmouthing to Friends

❏ No Contact with Kids

❏ Too Much Contact

❏ Arguing Around Kids

❏ _____

❏ _____

❏ _____

❏ Marital Name

❏ Real Estate Investments

❏ Pension/Retirement Accounts

❏ Stocks, Bonds, Etc.

❏ Household Furnishings

❏ Other Marital Property/Assets

❏ Business Assets

❏ Cars

❏ Loans

❏ Credit Card Bills

❏ Mortgages

❏ Other Debts

❏ Spousal Support

❏ Taxes

❏ His/Her New Relationship

❏ Your New Relationship

❏ Poisoning Family Relations

❏ _____

❏ _____

❏ _____

ow Conflicts Affect Children

Divorce can make life a real pressure cooker. Parents try to work out their conflicts and start a new life with half as much money. During the time when children need more support and nurturing, parents often have less time and energy to give them. In addition, children are often forced to contend with frightening displays of rage and accusations. In many cases, embittered parents simply fail to shield their children from parental problems and emotional chaos. Children are severely traumatized when they are forced to witness, and even encouraged to join into, the bitterness and bad-mouthing. In the long run, parents discover that this backfires and are heartbroken when their children turn against them.

The most agonizing problem for children occurs when their parents involve them in their problems. The conflicted loyalties children feel when their parents compete for their affection and allegiance often intensify all of their other feelings. No matter how bad the family was, children typically feel it gave them more support and protection than they have in a divorce situation.

Another effect of the hostilities is that a majority of non-custodial fathers tend to withdraw and visit infrequently despite the critical importance that staying involved has to their children. Surveys have shown that only 16 percent of children see their father as often as once a week! One-fourth of all children lose contact completely with their father. Children who are used to seeing a parent every day experience a deep sense of loss when forced to wait weeks between visits. Infrequent and erratic visits deepen the sense of rejection that children feel.

As their parents get caught up in their own stress, children feel abandoned. They may develop fantasies that their parents will reconcile and end their suffering. When that doesn't happen children become angry, sometimes to the point of explosive rages. Children just follow their parents example.

Because they want an intact family, children hate going from one parent's house to the other's. Parents often misinterpret this as the child not wanting to leave them to be with the coparent, rather than realizing that the child is torn between both parents. You will probably find that your children have difficulty expressing their unhappy feelings about not having the family they once knew because they fear hurting you.

Some of the other reactions that are common among children who are feeling the loss of their family are tearfulness, moodiness, restlessness, and difficulties with sleeping and concentrating. They become fearful that their basic needs won't be met, or that they'll have no one if their parents' emotional or physical health fails. Half of all children surveyed say that their parent's divorce "completely disrupts" their lives.

Forty percent of all children growing up in America today will suffer through their parents' divorce. And one of every six children will go through two divorces. The breakup of a child's family puts them into a period of incredible stress and emotional turmoil. How the parents handle conflict determines the degree of distress they will experience.

I Want To Protect My Children

List your top 10 reasons to learn new skills for resolving conflicts. Some examples given by others include:

- ◉ better example to my kids
- ◉ more time to do other things
- ◉ to feel less hassled all the time
- ◉ not as much money spent on lawyers

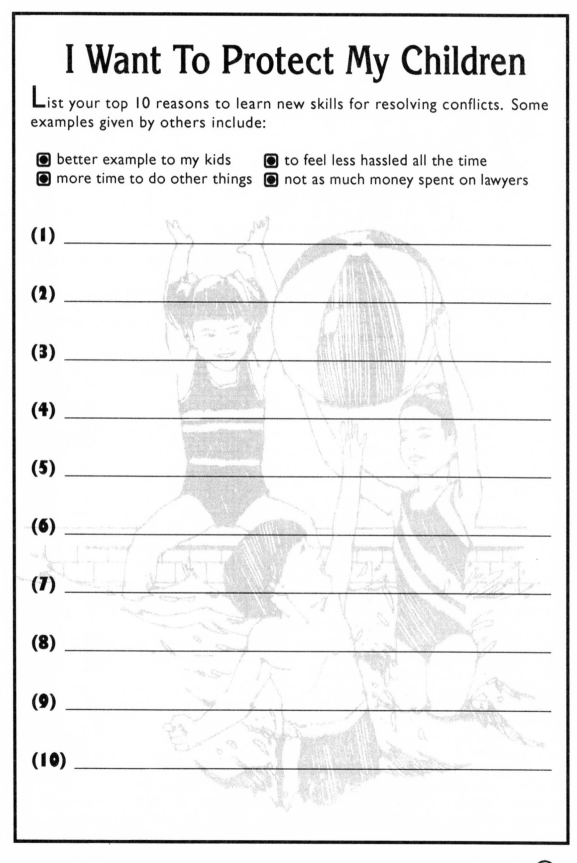

(1) _____

(2) _____

(3) _____

(4) _____

(5) _____

(6) _____

(7) _____

(8) _____

(9) _____

(10) _____

PITFALLS TO COMMUNICATION

There are two patterns of communication that people can use. One pattern leads to successful dialogue which results in a satisfactory outcome for both parties involved. The other pattern kills any chance of having a constructive discussion. Any type of verbalization that does not lead to a mutually satisfactory conclusion is doomed to failure.

Communication begins to collapse when someone becomes judgemental. One form of being judgemental is to become critical. Everyone knows the sting of being criticized, and how they tend to become defensive in their response. When someone has done something that you don't like, your natural tendency is to think that you need to provide them with the appropriate amount of criticism in order for them to learn the error of their ways. But then you are surprised when the other person reacts negatively to your judgement of them.

Another form of judgemental communication involves ridicule. This can occur when you call someone a name or belittle their position on an issue. For example, calling someone a "liar" is like pouring gasoline onto a fire. The conversation is likely to explode into an angry exchange that is totally destructive.

Whenever you tell another person what they have done is wrong, stupid, harmful, etc., you will elicit a defensive reaction from them. They may counter-attack and list the top 100 things they think you have done wrong. They will certainly justify their actions as being perfectly proper. They could clam up and seethe inside. They may shift into a display of righteous indignation, unable to comprehend how you could be treating them this way after all they have done for you. They might explode into a rage. It is unlikely that you will find any of these reactions very satisfactory.

Once an individual becomes flooded with negative feelings, they will remain physically stressed and stuck in that emotional turmoil for at least 30 minutes. Until these feelings

are resolved the person will have a negative attitude. This can cause them to become overly sensitized to slights or criticisms in other settings as well, resulting in difficulty relating to co-workers and friends.

Another pitfall can occur if you try to impose your solution on another person. Frequently you think of a way to solve a problem, but the other person rejects your idea. Remember that the only solution that is "right" is the one to which both parties agree. If you try to press your solution, it will only precipitate a power struggle and more frustration. Unless both people are getting what they want, it will never be a mutually satisfactory solution.

After battling it out for awhile, one person finally will have had enough and will walk off saying, "I'm not going to take this anymore!" They will then stonewall the situation, perpetuating a cold war in which there is no hope of reaching a resolution because there is no more opportunity to talk about the problem.

My Pitfalls

I feel criticized in conversations with the coparent when they say things to me like:

(1)

(2)

(3)

The coparent seems to react very negatively if I say things to them like:

(1)

(2)

(3)

When I think back on our arguments, I can remember how we each contributed to the fighting in the following ways:

❏ **Criticizing**　　❏ **Name-calling**　　❏ **Analyzing**

❏ **Evaluating**　　❏ **Demanding**　　❏ **Threatening**

❏ **Questioning**　　❏ **Moralizing**　　❏ **Advising**

❏ **Avoiding**　　❏ **Pacifying**

THE SOLVE METHOD
FOR RESOLVING CONFLICTS

Y ou *can* resolve the conflicts that will inevitably arise during your divorce. That is not to say that you will. The determining factor will be whether you learn to use the skills of the SOLVE method for problem negotiation and resolution.

"But what if the other side is impossible to deal with?", you ask. You have found them "impossible" because you have been using your old patterns for dealing with problems. You do not know what results you will get when you apply these new skills.

Learning to use these skills at this time is dependent on how well you are working through the emotional phases of your divorce. If your feelings are so strong that they interfere with your ability to have any kind of rational dialogue, then you need to work on your emotional issues first. If you have problems when you try using these skills, revisit Chapter 3 to get some additional help in managing the feelings that can be so disruptive during the divorce.

The S • O • L • V • E Model of Conflict Resolution

S chedule. When problems occur, one or both of the coparents can have powerful feelings arise. In order to resolve their differences in a business-like manner, the coparents need to schedule a time to discuss the issue when they are calmer. Stop and schedule another time if the conversation erupts.

O utcomes. In order to be able to resolve a conflict it is essential to know what each parent thinks will best meet the child's needs. Focusing the discussion on the outcome that each parent believes will accomplish this clarifies all of the ingredients that will need to be included in a solution. Therefore, it is important to specify what you *do* want, not what you *don't* want to happen in the future.

L istening. The only solutions that work are ones that are mutually satisfactory. Both people need to get most of what they want. Thus, what is required is that each person listen to the other so that they understand what that person needs in order to arrive at an agreement.

V erbalize Solutions. With both of the coparents' positions in mind, possible solutions need to be discussed. Several proposals will have to be considered before one is found that meets the needs of all the people involved.

E valuate. Even the best ideas will need to be refined as the people see how they actually work. Hence, it is wise to schedule a time to review the agreement so that any adjustments can be discussed. The process repeats itself as the outcomes of each person are listened to, and revised solutions are verbalized until a new agreement is reached.

Putting the SOLVE Model
Into Practice

Read through the example below and begin to develop your understanding of how to resolve conflicts.

This is a conversation between coparents who have practiced using the SOLVE model for a few months. They feel that the SOLVE model dramatically improved their communication skills.

Imagine how you will be able to use this process to resolve your conflicts after you have learned the skills involved.

S = SCHEDULE.
Father to Mother, "Mary, I'd like to talk about having mid-week visitation with the kids since they are now busy on Saturday mornings with sports. Could we talk one night next week about this?"

O = OUTCOME. Phone conversation one night the following week:
Father, "Thanks for calling. I'd like to start with both of us sharing our thoughts about how the kids' sports schedule is effecting our time with them. I'm feeling like I don't have enough time to talk with the kids since they started having games on Saturday mornings. I'd like to have a night during the week to spend some time with them. What do you think?"

Mother, "I know that we both want what's best for the kids, so I'd like us to think about how to avoid creating problems with the children getting their homework done."

L = LISTENING.
Father, "So you think that there won't be enough time for them to get their homework done if they spend some time with me on a week-night?"

Mother, "That's right."

V = VERBALIZE SOLUTIONS.
Father, "What if I picked them up after school and made sure that during our time together they got their homework done? Actually, that would give me a chance to see how their schoolwork is coming along. Would you agree to my spending a week-night with them if I worked with them to get their homework done?"

Mother, "I'd agree as long as you got them home for their regular bedtime."

E = EVALUATE.
Mother, "Let's try it for a month and then talk again after we've had a chance to see how well it works out."

Father, "It's a deal. Let's try this for the next four Wednesday nights."

SOLVE — SCHEDULE A TIME, PLACE & TOPIC TO BE DISCUSSED

How you initiate a discussion is very important. It can create an expectation that you genuinely want to discuss a problem and arrive at a mutually satisfactory agreement. To accomplish this, your attitude needs to be one you would use if you were talking to a co-worker about taking care of business at a job site: matter of fact, respectful, clear about your objectives, and willing to have a give and take type of discussion.

If your attitude involves believing you have the power to get your way without taking the coparent's needs into consideration, you will find that your win is short-lived. The other person will rather quickly sabotage the solution that you have imposed. Remember that to get what you want you must have the cooperation of the other person.

If you approach the situation with a defeatist attitude, you have a belief system that says you are going to come out on the losing end no matter what. With that approach in mind, you will try to please or appease the other person in the hope that they will treat you kindly when they decide how to handle the problem. They **WON'T!** Human nature is such that people tend to think of themselves, so if you don't stand up for yourself you may be taken advantage of and resentments will build.

To initiate a constructive conversation designed to address a problem and to solve it, start by adopting the win/win attitude. With the same tone of voice and choice of words that you would use in any business situation, tell the coparent that you would like to schedule a time and place to work out a mutually agreeable solution for an issue that has arisen.

Then tell the person specifically what you want to work out with them. First, have a non-judgemental description of the problem, being very careful to separate the person from the problem. Make an objective statement that is designed to give them feedback, not put them down.

Second, describe the behavior that occurred in terms specific enough that the other person can understand how their behavior adversely affected you. Share with the other person how their behavior cost you money or time, harmed your relationships, and/or interfered with your ability to function effectively in your life. Remember to avoid blaming and criticism by approaching them as if they were a co-worker.

It is important to focus the upcoming discussion on finding solutions to be able to work the issue out using a different behavior in the future. Although problems have obviously occurred, you want to avoid getting into an argument over who was at fault. Instead emphasize that you are seeking an opportunity for finding a resolution for the future.

How to Schedule Your Conflicts

Make the corrections that would improve the approach in the following example:

Wife: *"Damn it, you're late bringing the kids back from visitation again. You have no respect for my time at all. I'm not going to put up with your irresponsibility anymore. I'll just keep you waiting to pick up the kids next time and see how you like it!"*

Wife: _____

_____

_____

_____

See how your approach compares to the one provided below:

Wife: *"I'd like to find a time to talk to you on the phone about one or the other of us being late in bringing the kids to the drop-off point. I know that we both have busy schedules and we both have things come up that we can't control.*

But lately it's been causing some difficulties. I had to wait 35 minutes this week and 20 minutes last week. When that happens it throws my schedule off with the kids because I often have something planned for all of us to do together.

Neither of us want to sit around waiting for a long time. I'd like to find a solution that is mutually agreeable to both of us so that we can prevent a problem in future exchanges of the kids. When could we talk?"

Now write out one of your attempts to initiate a discussion that failed to gain any positive response:

_____

_____

_____

_____

Then rewrite how you have learned to schedule a time, place and topic to be addressed. Include a non-judgemental description of the person's behavior and how it affected your life.

_____

_____

_____

_____

s**O**LVE — OUTCOMES

ASK FOR WHAT YOU WANT

After you have scheduled the discussion, take some time to sit quietly and reflect on the results you would like to achieve. Identify an outcome that solves the problem by specifying what would be done, in what time frame, and within what guidelines.

Picture various possible outcomes that might solve the issue. Hear yourself explaining the details of each plan, including the pros and cons. Get a feeling of confidence in your ability to stay focused on creating solutions by thinking about various scenarios of how things could work out better from now on.

Remember that you cannot solve a problem that occurred in the past. No one can change what has already happened. So any discussion of who was to blame is going to be non-productive. The power to change things lies in getting the desired results when a similar situation next occurs.

How do you get someone to agree on changing things for the future, especially when they are probably unhappy with you at the present time? You will need to convince them that you are not trying to blame them or shame them. You simply want to agree on having a different result in the future.

To get someone to resolve a conflict:

- You will need to approach them with quiet dignity, conveying the message that you have respect for yourself and for them.
- You want them to listen to your problem, and you express a willingness to listen to their view of the situation.
- You develop the courage to express your needs knowing that they are likely to have an initial reaction that is defensive.
- You remain committed to using a communication process in which both people have the opportunity to create a solution in which their needs are met.

Prepare yourself for 10 defensive responses before the coparent realizes that you are serious about finding a solution. Do not get hooked into reacting to their attempts to attack you, to sidestep the issue, to question the validity of your position, or to withdraw from the discussion. Simply restate the outcome message that you had prepared before getting into the discussion.

An outcome message is a statement of the problem behavior, how that behavior is adversely affecting you, and a request to find a mutually agreeable new behavior to use in the future. Once you assert your outcome message, stop talking and start listening. You will have to cycle back and forth by asserting your outcome message and then listening to the other person's point of view several times before you get to the negotiation phase of the discussion.

Be persistent and you will find a mutually satisfactory solution.

How To Ask
For The Outcome You Want

Your desired result is a change in **behavior** that is mutually acceptable, not a continuation of the power struggle about who is right and who is wrong. Write down a non-judgemental description of the behavior which led to your having a problem. Then add what you would like to have happen differently in the future.

_____
_____
_____
_____
_____

Now read what you have written. Are there loaded words? Did you accuse the person of being wrong, bad, stupid, immoral, etc.? Did you suggest that their motives, attitudes or character are such that they intend to be hurtful? **Cross out anything in the above statement that is critical of the other person.**

You will have to be prepared to restate your position 10 times before the coparent's defensiveness, hostility, mistrust, and aggression has subsided. Write down the essence of your message so that you can restate it in 3 short sentences or less. Be specific when stating what you want to happen in the future.

_____
_____
_____
_____
_____
_____
_____

Now repeat the following sentence to help you stay focused on a positive communication process:

" And I'm willing to listen to what you need in order for the two of us to be able to find a solution that will work out satisfactorily for both of us next time."

SO L VE — LISTENING

To The Other Person

Listening is more than just hearing what someone says to you. It involves a three step process to comprehend the information that someone is trying to give you.

1. The first step is the restating back to the other person what you heard. This reflective listening will test whether or not your understanding of what was actually said is accurate.

2. Most of the time the other person will correct your initial understanding. Therefore, in the second step you will have to restate several times what they've said before they are satisfied that you "got it." They will also add several other bits of information that they want you to understand.

3. The third step in listening involves noting how the other person feels about what they are telling you. By also making a statement that reflects what you think the other person is feeling you will diffuse their pent-up emotions.

Problems in the listening process occur at every step. Often we are not really paying attention to what someone is saying. Therefore, we do not accurately understand their message and make responses based on faulty data. At other times our feelings are aroused by how we evaluate what has been said to us, and we allow our emotional impulses to rule our reactions. In either case, our responses do not lead to a constructive conversation.

To be a good listener it helps if you have a purpose for listening. If you are having a conflict with someone, your reason for listening to them is to be able to understand what they need in order to resolve the problem. In order to get what you want for your half of the win/win outcome, you will have to be sure the solution includes their getting what they want as well.

There are other important elements in effective listening. First, suspend your initial tendency to jump in with your judgements about what is being said. If you are only listening in order to gather ammunition for your rebuttal, you will be contributing to escalating the conflict. Instead, tell yourself that *you do not have to agree with someone's position in order to understand it.*

Second, do not interrupt with your own ideas, denials, or defenses. Reflective listening slows the communication process down and gives both of you time to calm yourselves before you respond to what is being said.

Third, when you begin to use reflective listening, start by telling the other person that you want to say back what you heard in order to be sure that you understand what they said.

Finally, keep the non-verbal communication positive as well. Face the other person and maintain good eye contact. Never allow yourself to be distracted by the TV or anything else. Maintain an attitude that shows that you want to keep a positive tone in the conversation.

Listening For Solutions

 Write down what the coparent says to you about a specific problem that gets you hooked into a conflict instead of a conversation.

_____

_____

_____

_____

 Write down a reflective listening response that uses some of the coparent's own words and feelings to summarize their message:

_____

_____

_____

_____

Do you think if you actually said your reflective listening response the coparent would feel you had understood their point of view? Or do you think they would find your response defensive or critical? Rewrite your response to eliminate any negative feedback so that when you read it you think it would be acceptable to the coparent:

_____

_____

_____

_____

To be sure that you know what the coparent wants in order to solve the problem, complete this sentence: "So if I understand your position on this issue, what you want in order to resolve this is ...

_____

_____

_____

_____

_____

SOL**V**E — VERBALIZE SOLUTIONS

To arrive at a resolution you must know what each person wants to have happen in order to be reasonably satisfied with the outcome. Having stated your concerns and listened to the other person's perspective, you now have enough information to begin to offer positive proposals.

A positive proposal is a possible solution that you are offering to determine if it meets the needs of both people. It should identify the issues involved for each person and describe how the proposed new behaviors could result in an acceptable solution. Usually this brainstorming process requires creating a series of new options as each proposal is considered and more is learned about what is needed to achieve a fully acceptable solution.

Some rules about making positive proposals include a prohibition against critical judgements. This type of evaluation curtails creativity by making people defensive. If you don't think an idea will work, make a counter-proposal that you think will address all of the key concerns. Don't ask for clarification, just use reflective listening. Don't let anything stop the process of creating new possibilities.

Another rule is to avoid thinking that there is only one solution that will work. There are always many options and you will be surprised at the many ways you will find to get everyone's needs met. If you start to feel stuck, get into some zany ideas. Making

some light-hearted suggestions will help relax the discussion and foster the creative process without belittling the other person. This brainstorming gets the ideas flowing, although at first they may be incomplete. Take the best parts of each idea and keep adding to them until they satisfy both people's needs. Continue to make positive proposals until an agreement is achieved.

If you get stuck, do not lapse into judgement or evaluation. Go back to defining the needs by restating your understanding of what each person wants. Ask the coparent what alternatives they would propose to meet these requirements.

If feelings start to run high, you can bring them back down to the normal range by reflective listening. Keep reflecting the other person's feelings until they recognize that you really do understand their side of the experience. Eventually they will calm down. Briefly restate your feelings that you do want to find a solution which meets their needs as well as your own. Suggest that it might help to sleep on it, and schedule another time to resume the brainstorming.

When you do reach an agreement, write down the specifics of who will do what and when.

How To Verbalize Win/Win Solutions

Think about a problem you are currently facing with the coparent for which you will be attempting to find a mutually agreeable solution. Add your ideas to the following list of techniques for maintaining your balance while asserting your position and listening to the coparent's point of view.

1. Exercise before the meeting

2. Avoid using alcohol or drugs to try to calm yourself

3. Write out your needs

4. Practice stating your position with a friend

5. _____

6. _____

7. _____

8. _____

Identify the obstacles you fear may block the negotiation process with the coparent. For every obstacle, write down a strategy for overcoming it using the guidelines given.

_____

_____

_____

_____

_____

_____

_____

Brainstorm some positive proposals you could suggest that might resolve the problem in a mutually satisfying way:

_____

_____

_____

_____

_____

_____

_____

_____

SOLV**E** — EVALUATE THE SOLUTION

As part of solving a problem, it is important to review how well the agreement worked out for all of the people involved. As with most things in life, you will learn how to make improvements as you actually implement a plan of action. For this reason, we strongly encourage you to set another time to meet after you have had an opportunity to discover how you could improve on the agreement.

Having an evaluation step also makes it easier to arrive at a solution that everyone is willing to try out. Knowing that the matter will be evaluated in the future allows each person to feel more comfortable committing to an agreement.

The topics to be discussed at this meeting could include the following:

- How do you think you and the coparent could improve in using the SOLVE process in future negotiations?

- What did you learn about that worked best when using the SOLVE model?

- In what area do you need additional practice when following the SOLVE steps?

- In what ways did the actual agreement work well?

- Was there anything about the agreement that did not work well for you?

- What positive proposals do you have for improving the agreement in the future?

Do not get upset if agreements do not work out at first. In fact, expect that at a minimum you will have to fine-tune them. People have busy schedules, conflicting priorities, and varying degrees of motivation that can interfere with implementing an agreement.

Be persistent. Keep trying to find a solution that will work. Listen carefully to why the coparent does not think the original idea worked out as successfully as you had hoped. Find out what they need to add to the agreement to improve it for them. Don't get discouraged. Assert your thoughts clearly and succinctly about how to upgrade the agreement.

With a mutual understanding of the problem in mind, start making positive proposals free of evaluation, criticism or references to past problems. Many times a lasting solution can only be reached by going through the SOLVE process several times.

Evaluating Agreements

W rite out your answers for the evaluation meeting ahead of time. In that way you will be well prepared for staying on the topic. Do not allow yourself to get caught up in a conversation that is not constructive.

1. In what ways did the actual agreement work well?

2. Was there anything in the agreement that did not work well for you?

3. What positive proposals do you have in mind for improving the agreement for the future?

4. In reviewing the SOLVE process, what do you feel would help make it work more easily in the future?

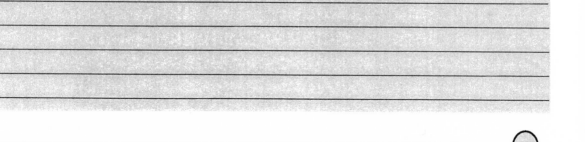

The SOLVE Model of Problem Negotiation and Resolution

S = **SCHEDULE.** When conflicts arise, one or both of the coparents can have powerful feelings. In order to resolve their differences in a business-like manner, they need to schedule a time in which they agree to address the specific topic in a calm manner.

O = **OUTCOMES.** When coparents do sit down to engage in a discussion, they focus on the outcome that they think will best meet their child's needs. They present that outcome in a positive manner free of blaming, criticizing, or threatening.

L = **LISTENING.** When a coparent presents the outcome they would like to achieve for their child, the other coparent responds by using a very important communication skill — REFLECTIVE LISTENING. This is an active listening response in which each coparent reflects back a summary of the words that each one used to describe their outcome. Thus, each parent gets the opportunity to be sure that the outcome they are suggesting is being accurately heard by the coparent.

V = **VERBALIZE SOLUTIONS.** In order to successfully resolve a conflict, a win/win solution must be agreed upon. This means that each parent's outcome must be taken into account so that the coparents both feel that the child's needs are being met. To arrive at a win/win solution, the coparent makes a series of proposals and alternatives they think will be mutually acceptable.

E = **EVALUATE.** After a win/win solution has been agreed upon, the coparents set a date and time to review how well their solution has worked. Any adjustments that they both agree to can be made at that time.

CHAPTER 5

Understanding How Children Get Sucked Into The "Black Hole"

Helping Children at Different Ages to Cope with Divorce

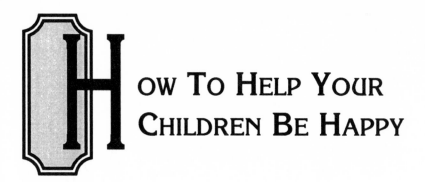

How To Help Your Children Be Happy

This divorce has been difficult for you. You're acutely aware of how painful it is when you get stuck in the pits and can't free yourself from the conflicts. That will give you a good idea of how your children feel about getting sucked into the black hole of divorce.

All parents want to protect their children from harm. This chapter will teach you how to do that. First, you will learn how to explain the divorce to your children. You'll discover how your children will probably feel and react to the breaking apart of their family.

By becoming aware of the danger signs, you can identify when your child is not coping well with the situation. More importantly, you'll learn what to do if your child is experiencing problems. With your help your children can successfully adjust to the divorce so that they can go on to have a happy life.

The following formula will make it easy for you to remember the important elements of what you can do to make your child happy:

Help Create Security

Actively Listen To Your Child

Protect Your Child From The Painful Conflicts

Provide Rules And Consistency

You Commit To A Better Life

EXERCISE:

Write down all the feelings, questions or comments you think your children might have when you talk to them about the divorce.

FEELINGS

QUESTIONS

COMMENTS

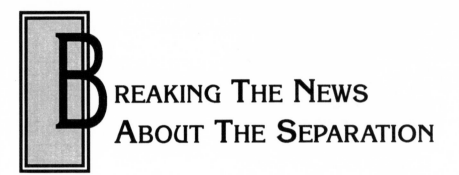

BREAKING THE NEWS ABOUT THE SEPARATION

For your children, life has always included Mom and Dad. Even if both parents were not equally involved in their day-to-day activities, they still had a sense of a two parent family. Even if they didn't hear or witness any serious fighting, it's hard to live in a family and not pick-up on the feelings which are floating around the house. Consider the following basic ground rules in discussing the divorce with your children.

- Think about what *they* need to hear (not all the details — but the big picture).
- Tell them in a way that minimizes their fears and insecurities (not blaming anyone, especially the children).
- Let them know there is an immediate plan (their life will continue and their needs will be met).

Ideally both parents should tell the children about the divorce together. This helps the children's sense of security that the people they are counting on will still be there to care for them. For the parents it is a good first step in beginning to provide positive coparenting. This will set the stage for a more healthy and successful adjustment for the entire family.

Discussing the divorce together with the children may be a difficult thing. However, letting them see that both of their parents have thought this through and have a plan for themselves and the children will add to everyone's sense of security and direction. Allow time for questions and try to answer them in an age-appropriate way. Do not become defensive, a reaction that tends to ignore the other person's feelings. When responding to your children's questions and concerns, put yourself in their place. Just think for a moment how scary, sad, insecure or angry your child may feel. Then respond in a way that shows you can empathize with your child's feelings. That means if your child says:

Child: Why did you make Daddy leave?

You would respond by saying:

Parent: It sounds like you're worried about Daddy and sad that he's gone.

This opens up the communication about the child's feelings rather than becoming defensive by trying to prove to the child that you didn't "make anyone leave."

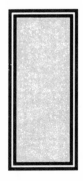

HOW TO DEAL WITH YOUR CHILD'S FEELINGS

Write out your positive responses to these examples. Remember to use empathy when you respond.

A. Child: *Who's going to take me to Boy Scouts now?*

_____

_____

_____

_____

B. Child: *Was Mommy mad at me because I wouldn't get ready for school?*

_____

_____

_____

_____

C. Child: *Will I still be able to go back to Camp this summer?*

_____

_____

_____

_____

D. Child: *Why did you always fight so much?*

_____

_____

_____

_____

HOW CHILDREN REACT TO DIVORCE

Parents who are aware of what to look for are better prepared to help their children deal with the divorce. Age, sex, stage of development, personality characteristics, shock of the change and family dynamics all play a role in how your child will handle the divorce. The following are some general verbal and non-verbal reactions that are observed in children of divorce.

Anger/Hostility
- Blaming one parent for the other one leaving
- Acting out at school and home, verbally and/or physically

Eating Problems
- Increased appetite/loss of appetite
- Demand for treats and "goodies" as a sign of love
- Digestive disorders/more stomach aches, etc.

Loss of Interests
- Drops out of activities; lack of energy
- More self-conscious around other people
- Won't be away from home for any length of time

Lying and Fabrications
- Telling stories about one parent or the other
- Making up fantasies about how life will be
- Manipulating the parents' for attention

Poor Sleep Habits
- Increased use of sleep as an escape
- Anxious and disrupted sleep (insomnia)
- Possible bed-wetting or need to sleep with the parent

Quiet and Withdrawn
- Spends more time alone
- Refuses to acknowledge anything has changed
- Won't let friends know about the divorce

School Problems
- Poor performance, forgetting assignments, lack of interest
- Trouble with teachers/authority figures
- Fights with peers/need for attention

DANGER ALERT
EXERCISE

1. List any of the danger signs which are occurring frequently in your child.

_____
_____
_____
_____

2. Which danger signs don't seem to be getting better with time?

_____
_____
_____
_____

3. Indicate any *drastic* and/or *unpredictable* behavior change.

_____
_____
_____
_____

4. In what areas could you, as a parent, use some assistance in helping your child?

_____
_____
_____
_____

 Some changes in behavior can be expected when children are faced with their parents' divorce. However, parents should be aware of the danger signs on the previous page. Counseling for your children may be necessary to assist them in their adjustment to the divorce if you found any of these danger signs!

THE REAL INSIDE STORY ABOUT KIDS AND DIVORCE

Over 1,000,000 children are affected by divorce each year. Around 40% of children born since 1980 will experience their parent's divorce. These children experience adjustment problems years after the divorce has passed and 30-50% carry the scars as excess emotional baggage into their adult lives.

The following statistics from the research of Judith Wallerstein in her book, *Second Chances: Men, Women, and Children a Decade after Divorce* can provide you, as parents, with a better understanding of what your child will be experiencing. By gaining this insight you can help your child learn to cope with and counteract the negative fallout from the divorce.

- Children in divorced families have up to 3 times more emotional, behavioral and learning problems than those who have both of their biological parents in the house

- 50% are tearful and moody and 33% are clinically depressed

- 75% are worried that their basic needs will not be met

- 50% feel rejected by one or both parents

- 66% suffer from loneliness

- 33% are angry and 25% have explosive rages

- Young adults 18-20 years old whose parents divorced when they were younger are twice as likely to have problems as those children from intact families. These problems include:

  ◆ 65% have poor relationships with their fathers

  ◆ 30% have poor relationships with their mothers

  ◆ 25% are high school dropouts

  ◆ 40% have received psychological help

- 59% of adult children of divorce are likely to have troubled relationships and broken marriages

HELPING YOUR CHILD TO ADJUST

1. Think about some ways you can help your child with his or her problem areas.

_____
_____
_____
_____
_____
_____

2. Write down a variety of possible solutions that you could try to help your child adjust better to his or her new family situation.

_____
_____
_____
_____
_____
_____

3. Set up a time to discuss your concerns with your child. Write down some ideas you come up with in that discussion.

_____
_____
_____
_____
_____

H OW INFANTS AND PRE-SCHOOLERS REACT

One of the questions often raised by parents who are getting a divorce is: At what age will my child be least effected by divorce? The answer depends on the child, the circumstances of the divorce and the consistency which can be maintained in the child's life.

Infants and toddlers are, in some ways, the most and least impacted by their parents' divorce. Because they are the most dependent on their parents, they are directly effected by emotional changes and mood swings which their parents experience. If the parents are unavailable or too needy themselves due to the distress they are experiencing during the divorce, the child will feel emotionally abandoned. However, if the divorce occurs when the children are very young, they have less time to witness any destructive marital problems or conflict in their home. They are spared the initial impact of "the death of the family" since they haven't really developed a true understanding of what "family" means. But still, they too will be faced, at some point, with mourning the loss of a dream they never even had a chance to experience.

Children need to develop trust and consistency in these early years to successfully master the normal developmental stages (*i.e.* stranger anxiety, separation, trust issues, insecurities). During a divorce, they are apart from one or both parents more frequently due to changing lifestyles. Children react by showing signs of stress marked by fearfulness, anxiety, sadness, anger and an overall difficulty in adjusting to change. They often regress to earlier behavior patterns; wanting to be fed, taking a bottle, needing a diaper, thumb-sucking, temper tantrums, frequently crying and whining, and baby-talk.

Since this is the age of "magical thinking", preschoolers feel they can control whatever happens. They often feel responsible for the divorce even if they have been told repeatedly that they had nothing to do with it. If parents divorce when the children are pre-school age or younger, communication with the coparent is essential. For the child to develop a relationship with both parents, each one needs to be a caregiver and meet the child's needs on a regular basis. This will foster feelings of love and security in the child rather than anger and abandonment.

EXERCISES FOR PRE-SCHOOLERS

Under each of the categories below, there are examples of things which you can do to help your **pre-school child** cope with the divorce. Using these suggestions along with our own ideas, write down your action plan for helping your child.

ACTION PLANS:

 Consistency: Practice setting limits, regular bed-time routines, playtime, meals etc.

 Emotional Stability: Don't share all your adult feelings with your child; find a friend or counselor.

 Caregiving: Use familiar and quality caregivers and limit change; let them see family and friends on both sides.

 Access/Visitation: Provide for frequent access to both parents, regular visitation; put it on their calendar.

 Conflict Resolution: Minimize yelling and arguing with the child as well as the coparent.

 Listening: Set aside time each day to talk or play to let them express feelings.

Reassurance About the Future: Use a calendar and plan ahead; give them guidance.

 Answer Questions: Be age-appropriate; tell them both parents love them and will always be there for them.

OW ELEMENTARY CHILDREN REACT

As children begin their *elementary school* years they begin to form a better understanding of what "belonging" means. This is the time when they really start to make comparisons between themselves and other kids in their family, neighborhood and classroom. A strong family system gives a child the comfort and confidence to go out into the world and take on all the challenges it presents.

Some researchers suggest that children in this age group experience the most significant impact of their parents' divorce. Young school age children (ages 5-9) have strong emotional reactions. They tend to personalize the divorce believing that somehow they "caused" one parent to leave, especially if they have heard their parents fighting over them at some time in the past.

At this stage of development the child will also fantasize plans of how they can be the "super-hero" and rescue or reunite their parents. If this doesn't happen, the child feels they have failed and their self-esteem suffers.

Loyalty issues also play a part in the elementary school child's reaction to the divorce. They feel sadness and longing, often missing the parent who left regardless of the closeness of the relationship when they lived together. These children also become particularly sensitive and threatened that they may be abandoned by the other parent as well. They are afraid that they will be replaced by someone else including other children who will come into their parents' life. That is why they are reluctant to have their parents date or get involved with anyone too soon.

At this age, children are frequently caught in the middle when their parents divorce. They are sometimes asked to relay messages back and forth between the parents or answer questions about the other parent's life when they visit. Parents need to avoid putting their children in a position to take sides for or against their parents. Preserve their childhood and minimize negative information you communicate to them about the other parent. They have a right and a need to love both parents. Children must not be used (even unintentionally) as another weapon in their parents' divorce battle.

Exercise For Elementary School Children

Under each of the categories below, there are examples of things which you can do to help your **elementary school age child** cope with the divorce. Using these suggestions along with our own ideas, write down your action plan for helping your child.

 Consistency: Keep child in same school, activities, and friends.

 Emotional Stability: Protect child from phone conversations that involve the divorce.

 Caregiving: Parent informs caregiver so child doesn't have to.

 Access/Visitation: Keep coparent informed about activities and invite participation.

 Conflict Resolution: Have business-like discussions with coparent away from child.

 Listening: Watch videos on divorce and discuss with child. Encourage them to express their feelings.

 Reassurance About The Future: Let them know where they'll be living, that they can still do their activities (within reason).

 Answer Questions: Be specific and avoid blame. Reassure child they aren't responsible. Avoid mixed messages about reconciliation.

How Middle School Children React to Divorce

At this age a child thinks in "absolutes". Something is either black or white, good or bad. Therefore, they are faced with finding "fault" in one or both of their parents for the divorce. Often they develop strong feelings of anger toward the parent they feel caused the divorce. They tend to align themselves with the "good" parent who they perceive was willing to maintain the family. This is often the parent they choose to live with or with whom they choose to spend most of their time. Many times children become a "companion" for the parent to fill the void left by the other parent. Problems arise when roles become confused and children take too much responsibility.

A psychologist named Lawrence Kohlberg found that pre-adolescence is marked by the development of rigid, moralistic standards which effect how children relate to their world. Parents can expect rather dramatic reactions from children in the 9 to 12 year old range.

Close friendships with same-sex peers suffer when children are going through their parents' divorce. Trust issues arise and children begin to fear attachment and question whether or not they can count on anyone. Significant behavioral changes that occur can become permanent and should be monitored closely. Watch for loss of interest in school work, withdrawal, angry outbursts, fighting, and experimenting with smoking, drugs, and/or alcohol. Physical complaints may also surface in this age group. Kids feel ashamed and internalize their pain and fears resulting in headaches, stomach aches, and susceptibility to other illnesses.

Some children attempt to cope by becoming overly involved in activities outside of the home (schoolwork, sports, overnight sleepovers) to avoid dealing with the divorce. Parents may miss the signs of distress in children who are coping by focusing on something else. While this may first appear to be a functional way of dealing with what is happening to their family, they also need to deal with their feelings rather than bottle them up inside. At this age, children need to learn the communication skills that will allow them to express themselves constructively and not by means of emotional outbursts. As you're engaged in activities with your child, create a safe atmosphere for them to share their feelings. Encourage them to talk to you by using your listening skills.

EXERCISE FOR MIDDLE SCHOOL CHILDREN

Under each of the categories below, there are examples of things which you can do to help your **pre-adolescent child** cope with the divorce. Using these suggestions along with our own ideas, write down your action plan for helping your child.

ACTION PLANS:

 Consistency: Keep child involved with friends and family. Keep same rules and limits.

 Emotional Stability: Let them express feelings in appropriate ways (not destructive name-calling). Let them love both parents.

 Caregiving: Make sure needs are met so they can feel secure. Minimize their time alone.

 Access/Visitation: Encourage them to see other parent. Don't give false hope about reconciling. Minimize exposure to parent's dating relationships.

 Conflict Resolution: Don't involve children in fight with coparent. Keep them from legal discussions or documents. Show respect for the other parent.

 Listening: Give children a chance to share feelings. Mirror back child's feelings so they feel understood.

 Reassurance About The Future: Keep them focused on what they need to do in their own life.

 Answer Questions: Respond to their concerns without pulling them into the "blame game."

How High School Chidren React

To paraphrase Charles Dickens in the opening lines of *A Tale of Two Cities,* "It was the best of times, it was the worst of times . . .". This seems to be an accurate description of the high school years when teenagers are experiencing the emotional struggle necessary to move from childhood into adulthood. If faced with their parents' divorce during this period of their life, children sometimes respond with feelings ranging from anxiety to relief. This depends upon how much marital conflict they have been exposed to and what type of relationship they have with each parent.

Since teens are often self-centered, their immediate concerns are about how their parents' divorce will effect *their* lives. They may worry about whether they will have to move, or lose some of the financial security they have come to count on. Relationships with peers are very important to them and they fear they may be damaged or destroyed by their changing family life.

Parents sometimes try to rely on their teenagers when they are going through the divorce process and want them around more often. Unfortunately this comes at a time when teenagers are moving toward separating from the family in order to become more independent and self-sufficient. Some children react by constructing emotional barriers to protect themselves from the turmoil.

Others become more dependent and vulnerable, relying too much on one of their parents.

Adolescents who see their parents struggling with the conflicts and emotional pains of the divorce may become frightened about their own ability to form healthy relationships in the future. They are anxious to distance themselves from their parents' conflicts. In an effort to prove themselves, they rush into inappropriate and overly intense, intimate relationships. These children are trying to replace their family relationships (which they feel have failed them) with another relationship with a boyfriend or girlfriend. These teenagers are also confused and upset by the competition with their parents who may begin dating.

Teens normally challenge authority during these high school years. Often, their parent's divorce causes them to try to assume too much independence, thus multiplying the conflicts. They often feel angry, vulnerable and unable to get the support they need to successfully move on in their lives. Parents too, struggling with their own needs during the divorce, can find it overwhelming.

EXERCISES FOR HIGH SCHOOL CHILDREN

Under each of the categories below, there are examples of things which you can do to help your **adolescent child** cope with the divorce. Using these suggestions along with our own ideas, write down your action plan for helping your child.

ACTION PLANS:

 Consistency: Keep same rules and expectations about school, dating, friends, etc.

 Emotional Stability: Be firm when they challenge authority. Reassure them they are not "doomed to failure."

 Caregiving: Let your kids feel connected. Do little things to take care of them.

 Access/Visitation: Schedule time with you and others. Have fun and build memories.

 Conflict Resolution: Show your child how to solve problems. Respect one another's needs.

 Listening: Make time alone (e.g., a car ride). Let them talk and avoid judgement. Show your interest in them.

 Reassurance About The Future: Encourage them to share any fears about the future. Focus on how they can be successful.

 Answer Questions: Respond to their concerns without pulling them in to the "blame game."

How Adult Children React

It can be shocking to realize that 59% of the children whose parents divorce will experience troubled relationships and broken marriages. Parents sometimes decide to wait until the children have graduated from high school or gone off to college to get divorced. Doesn't this seem like an appropriate time to make the break since their lives are changing anyway? While it is true that they are at a point of transition, this in itself evokes a tremendous amount of insecurity and self-doubt.

They count on things to remain constant at home so they can be free to explore "strange new worlds" while still feeling grounded. Many college counselors presenting orientation programs to parents advise them not to go forward with a divorce if at all possible as soon as their child leaves for college. This can cause children to feel as if they were responsible: **(a)** for keeping their parents in an unhappy marriage for years, or **(b)** for abandoning their family and causing it to fall apart.

As the adult child tries to establish his or her own life they are faced with questions about the values they were taught in their "first family." Adult children will also need to construct a separate relationship with each of their parents after the divorce. This can become strained if they are drawn into the conflict by either side. Parents need to set their children free to establish whatever contacts they want to have with each of their parents. Relationships between siblings in a divorced family can also be damaged if either of the parents try to forge an alliance with one over another.

Hopefully, if the divorce has minimal conflict, the adult children will be able to get the type of relationship they need with Mom **and** Dad. Most of the problems with divorce which are present when the children are younger have disappeared. You won't have the same things to fight about, but you can still involve your children in your arguments. Adult children will have significant events in their lives at which they will want both parents to be present (*i.e.* college graduation, wedding, childbirth, holidays). Many of these events will be ruined for them if the hostility continues.

As parents you can learn to participate with minimal tension and disruption, rising above petty conflicts for the love of your children

EXERCISE FOR ADULT CHILDREN

Under each of the categories below, there are examples of things which you can do to help your **adult child** cope with the divorce. Using these suggestions along with our own ideas, write down your action plan for helping your child.

 Consistency: Maintain regular contact with children. Stay involved in holidays, birthdays, etc.

 Emotional Stability: Deal with your own emotional needs and let children deal with theirs.

 Caregiving: Provide a home base. Don't expect them to stay; let them move on.

 Access/Visitation: Don't avoid visits with children and grandchildren because of coparent.

 Conflict Resolution: Resolve any disagreements. Never mention how they're like the other parent.

 Listening: Spend some one-on-one time with each child. Listen rather than preach at them.

 Reassurance About The Future: Be their fan club and tell them how proud you are of them.

 Answer Questions: Respond to their concerns without pulling them into the "blame game."

FACING FACTS ABOUT DIVORCE

In the Declaration of Independence certain inalienable rights were established by our forefathers. Among these are the rights to life, liberty and the pursuit of happiness.

I wonder if our forefathers took into consideration that one person's happiness may bring about another person's unhappiness and pain. This seems to be the case for children of divorce. Whether one or both of their parents choose the path of divorce, the children usually have little to say in the matter and yet experience the full impact of the decision. Five years after a divorce well over one-third of the children involved were significantly worse off than before, according to the research of Judith Wallerstein, author of *Second Chances: Men, Women, and Children A Decade After Divorce.* They were depressed and not doing well in school or with friends.

Not surprisingly, one-third of the children studied had witnessed intense bitterness between their parents during and after the divorce. When the family structure breaks down, children are at risk!

The family system is like a ladder the children must climb, moving up each rung of development from infancy through adolescence. The ladder is a secure base for their ascent into maturity. Divorce causes the ladder to collapse, and the child loses support for their social, emotional and academic progress.

Divorce compels changes in the structure of the family, leaving the children feeling frightened because the source of support and protection they depend upon is no longer intact. During divorce, the parents' problems almost always diminish their capacity to care for their children in all areas — disciplining, loving, playing, physical and emotional nurturing. Divorcing parents were found to spend less time with their children and to be less sensitive to their children's needs.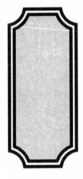

Children react to divorce with fear (*Who will take care of my needs? Who will take care of me? Will I get what I need from my parents?*). They often become angry as well, upset their parents' problems have destroyed their world as they knew it. While divorcing parents are able to see the possibility of a successful future, often the parents are so caught up in their own turmoil, the child understandably feels alone with no one to turn to for support.

Write a letter to help your child deal with his or her fear of the future. Include:

- How you think they are feeling
- How you are feeling for them
- What you hope for them in the future
- What you think they can do to help themselves
- What you are willing to do to help them

Dear

_____

_____

_____

_____

_____

_____

_____

_____

_____

_____

_____

_____

_____

_____

_____

_____

_____

_____

# SOME KIDS TURN OUT OK

While many children may still have serious adjustment problems years after their parents' divorce, research shows us that there are also some children who emerge as happy and successful. Therapists who deal with children of divorce emphasize the importance of helping the children get through the pain and crisis. They help them to see how life can be okay after the divorce. As parents, you too can encourage your children.

The main factors present in those children who were able to satisfactorily adjust to the divorce were:

◆ inner resources (e.g. good self-esteem)
◆ emotional support
◆ positive examples set by parents for rebuilding their lives
◆ the ability to overcome any negative examples set by parents
◆ parents who were able to *cooperate* in the task of childrearing

According to Clark W. Blackburn, General Director of the Family Services Association of America, "No real evidence exists to prove that children cannot turn out well when divorced parents disregard their own personal antagonisms and continue to act together in the best interests of the children."

Meet David . He's 10 years old and his parents are getting a divorce. His Mom and Dad sat him down in the living room and told him the news. He and his younger sister, Shannon, were both there and he said he wasn't all that surprised. David knew they were arguing. The parents told him that they loved him very much and that he had nothing to do with their decision to divorce.

His parents explained that he and his sister would stay in their house with Mom; Dad would be over a couple of times during the week to help him with homework and take him to his scout meetings. The weekends would be divided too, and every other one he would spend at Dad's new place. His Dad told him it would be his other home. David was a little excited since Dad had said he would get bunk beds for David's new room at his house. His parents told him he'd still go to the same school and be able to participate in his sports activities. Both his Mom and Dad would still take turns driving him and his friends. They would also try to attend his games just like they always had.

David was encouraged to express his feelings at anytime to either parent and to ask if he needed more time with either of them. Then the entire family made a pledge to get along and discuss any problems that came up so they wouldn't fight like some families do during a divorce.

YOUR POSITIVE SCRIPT

N ow write your own story of how you will create a successful divorce experience
for your children. Include the information you learned about the reactions and
concerns at various ages. Describe how you will develop their self-esteem, provide
emotional support, protect them from conflict, and be a good role model.

How To Make Your Child Happy

In our prescription for achieving a successful divorce, we have incorporated five key ingredients to help alleviate some of the negative effects of the divorce on your children. We refer to these ingredients as our **HAPPY formula:**

H Help Create Security for your child by reassuring him or her that their basic physical and emotional needs will be met. Children of any age or stage of development feel vulnerable when their family is splitting apart. Food, clothing, shelter, love and affection are basics which we take for granted. However, children sometimes fear they will be alone and abandoned when one of their parents leaves the home. Providing them with secure feelings will make them better able to cope with the emotional issues of the divorce.

A Active Listening is the communication skill which involves reflecting back what your child tells you they are thinking and feeling. Frequently, parents who are in the middle of a divorce become pre-occupied and their communication with their children can suffer. They may assume they know what and how their child will think and feel about the divorce. However, it is important that they take the time to really listen. This will build a closer relationship.

P Provide Rules with rewards and consequences so that your child will know what is expected and what will happen to them based on the choices they make. Anxiety and fear on the part of the children often accompany the news that their parents are getting divorced. They need to have consistency and order in their life as well as ground rules to follow which are appropriate and reasonable. Both parents need to establish these rules jointly whenever possible.

P Protect Your Child From The Parents' Conflicts and preserve the child's childhood by insulating them from involvement in the parents' problems, concerns, feelings and conflicts. Children of divorce are often forced to face the concerns and problems of adult life too early. One of the greatest gifts you can give your children is the memory of a happy childhood so they can draw upon it in their adult life.

Y You Commit to a Better Life for you and your child. In order to minimize the negative impact of the divorce on your children, you need to establish a business-like working relationship with your coparent. Together you can provide the love and nurturing that your children need and deserve.

Imagine you are in your child's shoes. Write down what thoughts and feelings your child might have in each of the 5 areas.

H Help Create Security:

A Active Listening to Your Child's Feelings:

P Provide Rules with Rewards and Consequences:

P Protect Your Child From The Parents' Conflicts:

Y You Commit To A Better Life:

Summary: What is Likely to Happen to Children Whose Parents Divorce?

What ultimately happens to the children depends to a great extent upon how well the parents do at learning to stop fighting and start resolving their conflicts. This is because the problem for almost all children of divorce is that they too are struggling to deal with negative feelings — sadness and anger toward their parents: anger at losing daily contact with one of their parents; anger if they lose their friends because they have to move; anger that there is less money; anger if their parents force them into loyalty conflicts; and anger at feeling powerless in the midst of it all.

Children of divorce often do not feel safe enough to express their angry feelings directly to their parents for fear of rejection. But in children as young as 2, temper tantrums and irritability are much more frequent in children whose parents are divorcing than in intact families.

Divorcing parents of children ages 3 to 6 report that they frequently have an unusual amount of difficulty getting their children to obey. Studies show that in addition to more tantrums and irritability, these children are also more moody, aggressive, anxious and restless.

Children in the 7 to 8 year old range frequently have reconciliation fantasies. But when the parents don't get their marriage back together, these kids are hurt and angry. Their pain doesn't always get better quickly. After five years, 50 percent of children whose parents divorced were still showing an array of negative emotions. For 25 percent of the kids, their symptoms had actually worsened.

The expression of anger can be intense in children ages 9 through 12, especially if the parents behave negatively toward each other. These children feel the need to try to take care of their parents. Obviously they are destined to fail in such endeavors, leading to a tremendous amount of frustration and anger.

Teenagers already have their share of hostility toward their parents and a divorce only amplifies their anger. Adolescents typically act out their negative feelings through behaviors such as drinking, drugs and sexuality. Forty percent to 60 percent of teenagers whose parents are divorcing report that they are experiencing emotional and behavioral problems.

By taking the time to work through the exercises in this chapter you have strengthened your ability to help your children (whatever their ages) to deal with the challenges presented by the divorce. In the years to come you and your children will reap the benefits of your determination to move on to a HAPPY life.

CHAPTER 6

Avoiding the Main Pitfalls that Affect Children

Protecting Your Relationship with Your Children During Divorce

PITFALLS AFFECTING CHILDREN

Children get into the pits when their parents are so busy fighting that their feelings get overlooked. The main areas of conflict involve time with kids, money matters and new dating relationships which add a whole new dimension to the scene.

When asked about why they wanted a divorce, many people say because they were tired of fighting. Good answer! But unfortunately not really an accurate one. Instead of stopping the fighting once you separate from your spouse, it often just shifts the focus to other issues. The way the fighting is conducted may also change after the separation occurs to one of litigation. This is a more formal type of fighting played out in a public forum using well paid hired guns. The aggravation and hostility is still alive and in some ways intensified, as other people are brought into the battle. In the worst divorce cases, parties take up opposing battle stations and force family members and friends to choose sides. They sometimes ask their children to act as jurors — forcing them to make adult decisions.

Therefore, the decision to get a divorce effects the entire family. The emotional impact of the actual separation is further compounded by the decisions which have to be made about: custody of the children, visitation arrangements, money issues including division of property and the family home, and new relationships.

Acceptable rules of etiquette around who, what, where, when and how these decisions will be made is frequently lacking. Instead, people "do divorce" like they've seen their own parents, relatives or friends do it. Unfortunately, those models have been far less than desirable and usually cause emotional damage for everyone involved.

The underlying principles for how to have a successful divorce are ones we learned as children. The Golden Rule of "do unto others as you would want them to do unto you" is part of the basic childhood curriculum that almost all of us receive. When conflict arises we expect pre-schoolers to learn to deal with conflict and resolve it in a healthy way. You probably remember learning these lessons yourself when you were a kid.

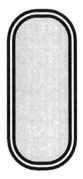

Sometimes, people in the middle of their divorce, appear to have forgotten everything they had been taught about fairness and sharing. By reading this book you are giving yourself a refresher course in how to live your life according to a good set of values.

FAIRNESS & SHARING EXERCISE

Issues of fairness and sharing arise in 3 major areas:

 Problems about children

 Problems about money (child support and marital property)

 Problems about relationships

You can apply the Golden Rule in dealing with these problem areas with your coparent.

What I can do to be fair about:

A. Sharing the children

_____

_____

_____

B. Dividing the money

_____

_____

_____

C. Bringing new people into my child's life

_____

_____

_____

The Changing Family: From The Children's Perspective

Your children found themselves in a family system they didn't choose but had to adapt to for their very survival. Without their input (and probably against their wishes) their family structure has now changed rather dramatically. You may have given them the best textbook explanation for why Mom and Dad are splitting up, but their dream of living in a "ma and pa family" has been shattered.

Your child feels confused about this turn of events and often experiences conflicted loyalties toward mom and dad. Depending on age and individual needs, they worry about how their life will be changed by the divorce. Here are some of the questions to address with your child:

- Who will your child live with?
- Will he/she still see the other parent? Grandparents? Other family members?
- Who was responsible?
- Will there be enough money to:

Eat?   Stay in their house?   Go to school?   Get clothes?

Continue their activities?   Go on vacation?   Get things they want?

Without answers to these questions, your child may feel scared and insecure and their self-esteem may suffer. Frequently children experience physiological symptoms, such as stomach aches, which are brought on by the anxiety and stress of their parent's divorce and the upheaval in life as they know it.

Your child may take the "blame" for the divorce and feel as if they should do something to fix it. If the child saw their parents fight a lot and secretly wished they would divorce, they'll feel particularly guilty as if by "magical thinking" they made it happen. Many children also begin to feel emotionally responsible for their parents. Your child may curtail their participation in some of the activities they have always enjoyed because they feel they need to be there for you. This is especially true when you rely too heavily on your child as a confidante and companion through the divorce process.

Children may feel particularly vulnerable during the divorce and try to hide their feelings rather than risk making things worse. Your child needs to be able to identify and express feelings to you and get the reassurance they need to face the changes in their family. This will minimize the long term damage.

C ircle those feelings which you think your child is presently experiencing about the divorce. If you have more than one child, do each child separately by using a different color pencil for each one. Add any other feelings you may have seen in your child as well!

LOST

ABANDONED

RELIEVED

ANGRY

GUILTY

ANXIOUS

SCARED

PAIN

EMBARRASSED

DISLOYAL

VULNERABLE

CONFUSED

HELPLESS

DESPERATE

INSECURE

HOPELESS

FRIGHTENED

SAD

PROBLEMS WITH CHILDREN

Children don't have any choice about their parents' decision to divorce, yet their lives are profoundly affected by that decision. Even when their parents have been openly fighting, many still say they want Mom and Dad to stay together. They long for a happy family and are threatened and insecure about how their life will be if their parents split up. Depending on their age, children often feel that they lose a significant part of their childhood.

Unfortunately, many parents only add to their children's fears by fighting over custody and visitation arrangements. When the marriage breaks up the parents feel lost and insecure themselves. In an effort to stabilize their lives they often try to put a tighter hold on the children. Parents focus on their own rights and needs concerning their children, but overlook those of the other parent. More importantly, they often lose sight of the needs and rights of their children.

In all but the rarest instances, children want and need a relationship with both parents. Just because the parents decide to separate, the child doesn't have to be split apart as well.

Having seen thousands of custody conflicts, it is not unusual for parents to argue over who "gets the kids", or yell at one another in front of their child at visitation exchanges. Holidays all too frequently become a nightmare for everyone. Equal time and "access" become a bigger priority for the parents than creating pleasant memories and traditions for the children. Kids get caught in the crossfire. The price they pay is a heavy one. They begin to experience more negative emotions than positive ones and are susceptible to difficulties in other areas of their life. These include poor school performance, lower self-esteem, negative interpersonal relationships and long-term psychological problems.

Parents need to realize that their children do not belong to either of them and are the responsibility of both of them. Parents can learn to resolve their own conflicts and agree on a parenting plan for their children. The SOLVE model which you've learned about in this handbook provides you with the tools to use to achieve this goal.

IDENTIFYING POTENTIAL CONFLICT AREAS

For each of the potential conflict areas below circle those which are problems for you. Next write down your position, as well as what you think the other parent's position would be on each of the conflict points.

	My Position:	Coparent's Position:
Visitation schedules		
Holidays		
Phone calls		
Activities		
Health Care		
Schoolwork		
Babysitters		

 AKING TIME FOR FAMILY FUN

Fun is the secret ingredient that provides balance to all of the serious concerns of family life. It's the stuff that makes for great memories of being together. The happiness that comes from having fun is the glue that bonds families together, especially during the tough times surrounding a divorce.

Ironically, if you ask most parents what they want for their children, they say it's for them to be happy. Yet most parents relegate play time as a family to one of the last priorities in their lives. Since parents are role models for every aspect of life, they are actually teaching their kids to feel guilty about having fun vs. being mature and doing what they "should".

Sometimes when parents do things with their kids, the experience is more like work than play. A sure sign of this is when there is a strong goal-orientation in the situation. The focus is on working to achieve something rather than just "savoring the moment".

Hopefully your children will be able to have fun with both of their parents. Don't tarnish their good times by interrogating them when they return to your home.

Another way to contaminate fun times is to impose a win-lose expectation into the activity. If it's competitive, someone is going to win and someone else is going to lose. And everyone is going to be tense while working to be the winner. If your fun times frequently result in looking back and feeling like a success or failure, then it was not really a relaxing, playful experience.

Set aside time for playing together just the way you would set aside money for something that you knew was important for your family's survival. Be sure that you pick

 something that puts emphasis on being active. The more sensory involvement — seeing, touching, hearing, feeling, smelling, tasting, etc. — the greater the amount of pleasure you will derive from the experience and the more renewed you will feel.

Let every family member contribute when deciding how to have fun. That means parents will need to let go of being "mature" and enjoy simple, sometimes silly activities. You'll be surprised how much fun you'll have. Remember, the amount of laughter will be a good way to gauge healthy play.

Helping your children to capture good memories about their childhood is one of the best legacies that you can pass on to them.

FUN ACTIVITIES TO SHARE

1) Circle the types of activities which you have shared with your child over the past month. Add any additional ones if not listed here.

holiday visit   going to a museum   telephone calls

time with relatives   going to work with the parent

meeting child's friends   field trip or activity   going to movies

eating at home together   listening to music together

going to pediatrician   playing a game   vacation

fixing something together   eating out   day long excursions

homework   shopping   reading a book together

making crafts together   doing a building project

one-on-one time with parent (without other siblings)

2) Discuss your list with your child and together choose 4 or 5 activities for you to share together. Write down what the two of you decided to do!

_____

_____

_____

_____

_____

MONEY CONCERNS

Parents need to help their children feel more secure as they go through the divorce process. Talking to your children about your money anxieties or relaying messages to the coparent through the children is not the recommended approach. This puts the children in a very difficult position thinking they have to make it OK somehow. Although this is impossible for them to do, they feel pressured to try. You need to work out a plan with your coparent so that, from the beginning, the top priority is making sure that the basic needs of the family can be met. Other financial concerns will be easier to negotiate if the groundwork of cooperation and responsibility is established and the basic needs are under control.

Two really cannot live as cheaply as one. So often when the divorce process begins, the money problems escalate as well. Because of the emotional turmoil which precedes the actual separation, family finances sometimes get neglected and neither parent trusts the other to manage the money any longer. In our society, the following is true:

MONEY = POWER + SECURITY

Once couples decide to divorce, each party feels a need to get their share and protect their interests. Sometimes their perception of their share doesn't take into account the joint debts and family obligations that still exist.

Each party wants to be sure they can afford to begin their new life. Their concerns are very real and practical ones. However, before they can begin a new life, each party has to complete any old business in their present family.

Conflicts over money occur when one parent begins to attribute all the money problems to the other parent; blaming them for:

(a) **not caring about the family**

(b) **having no concept of money**

(c) **being all wrapped up in themselves**

(d) **causing all the problems by leaving**

(e) **all of the above etc., etc., etc.**

Money arguments leave your children vulnerable and insecure, worrying about how they will be able to go on with their life (school, activities, friends) post divorce.

MANAGING MONEY PROBLEMS

Review the list of money problems often seen in the divorce process. Write down how you plan to handle each area, being as specific as possible.

1 Family rent/mortgage payment _____
_____
_____

2 Existing bills and debts _____
_____
_____

3 Household furnishings _____
_____
_____

4 Cars (and other toys) _____
_____
_____

5 Child support _____
_____
_____

6 Other child care costs (school, daycare, etc.) _____
_____
_____

7 Other money concerns _____
_____
_____

COPARENTING CONCERNS

Knowing how to "play fair" will really become significant as you continue to interact with your coparent. You and your "ex" have a major mutual interest — your child. More than likely that means each one of you will want to be present at the significant and important events in your child's life. These events can include: school plays or concert performances, sports events, award presentations, special field trips, religious ceremonies, graduation, marriage, birth of a grandchild, and all the various birthdays and family holidays throughout the years.

You may feel overwhelmed by the prospect of having to deal with this other person for years after you've divorced. First, be reassured that in time you will become more emotionally detached and the relationship with your child's other parent (the coparent), can take on a more cordial and business-like posture.

You can begin laying down the groundwork for a workable coparent relationship right now! Although the marriage didn't last, you need to recognize that the parental relationship has to continue for the sake of your child. What better legacy to give to your child than a happy homelife, even if his parents live apart. For a child, family means mom and dad — if not living together as a family unit, then at least not being warring enemies.

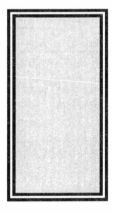

You also owe it to yourself to learn how to deal with your coparent fairly and with minimal hassles to you. It will make your life far less stressful. It takes two people to participate in order for an argument to occur. If you decide not to fight with your coparent and instead learn other ways to respond, then the arguments will stop.

We have worked with thousands of families who said to us that the fighting would never end. But they were pleasantly surprised when they discovered that by using our **SOLVE** method of conflict resolution the arguing gradually turned into constructive conversations.

ACTIVITIES WITH COPARENTS

Write down your ideas about how you would like to have these situations work out satisfactorily for you and your children in the future.

Event	Successful Outcome
School Activities	_____
Plays or Concerts	_____
Sports Events	_____
Award Presentations	_____
Field Trips	_____
Religious Ceremonies	_____
Graduation	_____
Selection of College	_____
Marriage	_____
Births	_____
Birthdays	_____
Illnesses	_____
Deaths	_____
Other	_____

NEW RELATIONSHIP CONCERNS

In the best of all possible cases, all of the major factors surrounding the divorce including child custody, visitation, financial matters and emotional issues would be settled before any new relationships are brought onto the scene. However, this is not usually the way it happens. Quite often, soon after the separation, at least one of the parties is seeing someone else on a casual or more committed basis. This adds an additional source of potential conflict to the already volatile and unstable family dynamics.

Even if the parties feel they have detached from one another emotionally, the introduction of another person often evokes feelings of competition and jealousy particularly when that other person is spending time with the children. Parents are just getting used to sharing their children's time with the coparent. Now they face the threat of also sharing them with a potential replacement that their ex-spouse has chosen.

This is even more explosive if this new person was someone who is seen as having "caused" or at least contributed to the family break-up. In these situations, it is very important for all parties to exercise maturity and restraint to eliminate a potentially damaging outcome for everyone, particularly the children.

From our work with families in the divorce process, we have seen children forced into relationships with mom or dad's "new friend" too soon, causing them to feel like they've somehow betrayed their other parent. In some cases, these new relationships have been severely damaged even before they got started. The other parent may verbalize their negative feelings about the "home wrecker" in very explicit terms to the children because of their own anger and emotional pain.

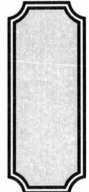

Children need to be protected from these conflicts as much as possible. Over time they will form their own relationships with many new people who come into their lives. Through it all, their mother and father will continue to occupy a unique and special place. For children, being able to have more people who care about them can be a positive benefit to balance out the loss they experienced when their original family broke up. But relationships with their parents' new friends need to start slowly. The child has to become secure by having time to adjust to their new family environment.

RATING
YOUR RELATIONSHIPS

1 Make a list of all the people who are a part of your life right now. Next to each name put a (**+**) if they are a positive source of support to you or your children in the divorce process. Put a (**-**) if they are a source of conflict to you or your children.

_____

_____

_____

_____

_____

2 Make it a point to sit down with your child and ask what they need from you to feel secure and connected.

_____

_____

_____

_____

_____

3 Write out a plan for balancing your time for socializing with what your child needs.

_____

_____

_____

_____

_____

_____

Burn-Out Concerns

Stress can effect children as well as adults. Research shows that people's physical and emotional health are effected by stress. Hans Selye, a well-known researcher and physician defined two types of stress — positive stress or eustress and negative stress or distress.

Some examples of positive stress might be: planning for a long-awaited family vacation, getting a new home, or even making a new set of friends. Negative stressors might be: leaving your old neighborhood, experiencing financial problems, or suffering a loss.

Your feelings about these two types of stressors are very different. However, the physiological responses by your body are similar. Your heart rate increases, your blood pressure is elevated, and you go on alert in an effort to prepare for any adaptations which the body may be required to make. This "fight or flight" syndrome is a model often seen in the interactions between coparents.

Some individuals engage in conflicts ("fight") verbally, and on occasion even physically, whenever they have to interact with their former spouse. There are other people who believe that avoiding any interaction ("flight") will make their life less

stressful. Unfortunately neither approach will eliminate the stress. The divorce situation will be stressful. The physical signs of stress include: headaches, twitchy eyes, constipation, diarrhea, stomach aches, fatigue, excessive sweating, cold hands and feet, teeth grinding.

For kids, there are a number of behaviors that are symptoms of stress: non-communicative, withdrawn, belligerent, uncooperative, poor concentration, day-dreaming, declining grades, nightmares, lying, exaggerating, clinging, often sick, overly sensitive, drinking or taking drugs.

To relieve stress in the family, there are several important steps you can take. First, eat properly by limiting junk food and being sure everyone eats nutritious meals. Second, get everyone out for some physical activities that they enjoy at least three times per week. Go to the park and kick a ball around or play on the swings. Finally, get enough sleep because everyone will cope much better when well rested!

STRESS
MANAGEMENT EXERCISE

1. What are the physical and behavioral signs of stress that you see in:

A. Yourself?

_____

_____

_____

_____

B. Your Children?

_____

_____

_____

_____

C. Your Coparent?

_____

_____

_____

_____

2. What can you do to reduce the stress level and avoid burn-out?

_____

_____

_____

_____

_____

MY SCHEDULE FOR STRESS-BUSTING

MONDAY:

_____

_____

TUESDAY:

_____

_____

WEDNESDAY:

_____

_____

THURSDAY:

_____

_____

FRIDAY:

_____

_____

SATURDAY:

_____

_____

SUNDAY:

_____

_____

CHAPTER 7

A Family Plan
For Staying
Out Of "Holes"

*Creating a
Happy New
Life for You
and Your
Children*

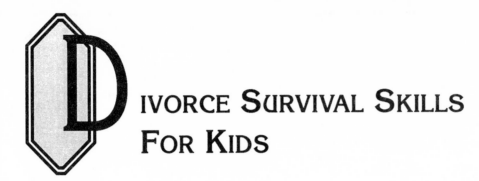

DIVORCE SURVIVAL SKILLS FOR KIDS

Helping your children deal with the divorce, as well as with life in general, requires providing them with the necessary tools and skills to handle whatever they might face. A familiar old proverb goes something like this: "If you give a man a fish, you feed him for a day; if you teach him how to fish, you feed him for life." This chapter is about teaching your children how to fish. Learning any new skill is hard especially under stressful circumstances. Providing a safety net helps give your children the courage to try new things. In the process you'll improve on your own survival skills as well.

Children learn more from what we do than from what we say. Being a positive role model for our children can be difficult under normal circumstances. It poses a challenge when you are experiencing your own pressures in the process of a divorce. But, by following some important guidelines, parents can help their child develop the confidence that they can face life's problems and get what they need.

1 st, meet your children's need for security by helping them to know they have two loving parents. Kids need to feel supported, loved, understood and appreciated no matter what problems their parents might be having.

2 nd, children need to be able to express their love for both of their parents. Regardless of how you may feel toward the coparent, children have the right to have their own feelings.

3 rd, you need to facilitate contact between your child and the coparent. Go out of your way to encourage calls and visits between them. This will allow your child to be reassured they are loved by both of their parents.

To interfere with a child's love for his parent is incredibly selfish and unfair. It will also backfire, because the child will come to deeply resent the parent who has interfered with one of nature's most powerful attachments. Just when you think you have it all together, you may find yourself dealing with a whole new set of emotional feelings and reactions. For both you and your children's sake, work on creating a positive and loving lifestyle based on a solid set of values to serve as a blueprint for family life.

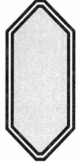

MAKING LOVE WORK
FOR KIDS AND COPARENTS

1 How I will meet my children's needs so they feel that they have two loving parents:

_____
_____
_____
_____
_____

2 How I will help my child to be able to express their love for both of their parents:

_____
_____
_____
_____
_____

3 How I will facilitate contact between my children and the coparent:

_____
_____
_____
_____
_____

THE RULES FOR HELPING CHILDREN

Basic training for life includes providing your children with the skills for managing their inner world of feelings and needs. It must also include preparing them to deal with the responsibilities and demands of the outside world.

There are six major areas that you will remember having worked on for yourself: Body, Mind, Spirit, Work, Love, and Play. These become the outline for your plan to help your children deal with the divorce process.

However, before your child can concentrate on developing new skills they need to be out of the "war zone" and in a "safe house" or houses. The following 10 principles can provide the ground rules for preparing your child for life after divorce.

THE 10 GROUND RULES
For Helping Children To Get Out Of The Pits

1. Make sure your children know they are loved by both parents.

2. Avoid bitterness, arguing and other negative behaviors.

3. Keep a positive outlook about the future and pass that on to your children.

4. Provide an example for your children of how to balance work and play.

5. Maintain a supportive network of friends and family in your children's lives.

6. Show your children how to deal with responsibilities and decisions in a fair and honest way.

7. Don't deceive yourself or your children by trying to excuse your contributions to problems by shifting blame to others.

8. Have your own ideas and opinions but be flexible and responsive to those of others.

9. Dare to dream and back it up with a realistic plan.

10. Believe in yourself and your ability to create a good life.

Once you establish these underlying principles, you have set the stage for helping your children deal with divorce and life thereafter.

APPLYING
THE 10 GROUND RULES

1 Think how your child would rate the following statements about the 10 Ground Rules on the previous page.

	Almost Always	Occasionally	Almost Never
1. I feel loved by both of my parents.	❑	❑	❑
2. I don't see much arguing.	❑	❑	❑
3. I think things will turn out OK.	❑	❑	❑
4. My parents show me how to balance work and play.	❑	❑	❑
5. I have a lot of people I can go to for support.	❑	❑	❑
6. My parents act fairly and honestly.	❑	❑	❑
7. My parents don't blame one another.	❑	❑	❑
8. My parents listen to my ideas.	❑	❑	❑
9. My parents are my "biggest fans."	❑	❑	❑
10. I believe my parents will create a good life for all of us.	❑	❑	❑

2 Now go back and ask your child to rate each statement. Don't get defensive! Use your reflective listening skills in order to keep the communication channels open.

139

HELPING CHILDREN REGAIN THEIR BALANCE

Divorce effects children in all areas of their life! Body, mind, spirit, work, love and play. As parents you will be called upon to help them deal in each of these areas.

BODY: Helping your child deal with the impact of the divorce on their body is an important place to begin. Children sometimes experience poor eating and sleeping. In order to minimize these reactions, maintain as much consistency as possible for your child. Prepare meals and establish schedules for bedtimes. This is true for all age children (even if the older ones do bend the rules from time to time). Maintain regular doctor appointments for check-ups even if life is hectic and a little overwhelming at times.

MIND: The thoughts and feelings which your children have as they begin to face the divorce will sometimes be frightening to them. Although you may think there is a general understanding and nothing more needs to be said, encourage them to talk about it. You may be surprised to find out that your children have jumped to false conclusions based on little bits of information. They can also have many fears and fantasies, neither of which help them work through the realities of the divorce.

SPIRIT: Many children lose hope when they find out their parents are getting a divorce. If they have any spiritual beliefs, these are shaken and sometimes they even feel ashamed about the whole thing. Provide some time for reflection and meditation and give them a place where they can renew their faith and hope in their future life after the divorce.

WORK: For children their work consists of performing in school and taking responsibility for their chores around the house. Frequently children in the middle of a divorce have problems with concentrating and completing tasks. Parents can help their children deal with these tendencies by showing an interest in their schoolwork, participating in teacher conferences, and helping establish the time and place which facilitates doing their work.

LOVE: When a family splits in two, children often feel like the love they will receive will be cut in half as well. They sometimes experience many more negative emotions within their family. Conflicts erupt between Mom and Dad, often over them. Children can be helped to deal with the divorce by giving them love from both parents. Encouraging them to reach out to other family members and friends can also help in meeting their needs.

PLAY: Childhood and play should be closely associated. When a family is going through a divorce, play may become even more important. Children often use play as an outlet to release their emotions. Giving your children permission to be children and have fun will help them cope as they face the serious business of divorce.

"BALANCE SHEET" FOR CHILDREN

S it down with each child to talk about their needs in Body, Mind, Spirit, Work, Love and Play. Include specific actions and interventions you will suggest they use to help them cope with the divorce in the 6 areas of their life.

1. Child's Name: _____

  a) Body: _____

  b) Mind: _____

  c) Spirit: _____

  d) Work: _____

  e) Love: _____

  f) Play: _____

2. Child's Name: _____

  a) Body: _____

  b) Mind: _____

  c) Spirit: _____

  d) Work: _____

  e) Love: _____

  f) Play: _____

THE ART OF GETTING YOUR KIDS TO TALK TO YOU

When a family is going through a divorce, the communication patterns can become even more distant and problematic. This is the case with children and their parents, regardless of where they spend the majority of their time. Communication patterns vary depending on the family members themselves. Research shows that even in families that are together, parents and children rarely talk to one another.

What's the reason for this breakdown in communication? Some of the reasons are obvious: busy family schedules, fatigue, frustrations with one another, and a lack of good communication skills. Sometimes parents shut down the channels of communication with their children by openly criticizing the other parent to the child. Another mistake is putting the child on the hot seat and pumping them for information about the coparent. Probably the worst thing you can do as a parent is ask your child to take sides in the divorce conflict. They will feel torn apart and resentful. While they may tell you what you want to hear, your child won't really be communicating with you.

Here is a brief communication lesson to help you better connect with your children. The main aspect of communicating isn't talking but listening. You each have two ears and one mouth — this is so you can listen twice as much as you talk. But what do you listen to if your children won't talk to you?

It may sound strange, but your children will begin talking to you once you listen. Listening involves:

HEARING — really tuning into what your child is saying both verbally and non-verbally. You can do this by concentrating and maintaining eye contact and not being distracted.

UNDERSTANDING — being compassionate, trying to interpret their feelings about what they said, being able to put yourself in their shoes. You don't have to always agree to understand their point of view.

GIVING A RESPONSE — feedback lets your child know you heard them and understand. This is active listening — reflecting back what you heard to show you "got it".

Now you can use the **HUG** (*H*earing, *U*nderstanding and *G*iving a response) method of communication with your child. You will both feel better.

HUG YOUR KIDS
SO THEY WILL TALK TO YOU

1 Write down something your child has said to you recently about a neutral topic. Now apply the **HUG** method and write out your response.

_____

_____

_____

_____

_____

_____

_____

_____

2 Now write down something your child has said to you about the divorce. Apply the **HUG** method in this more difficult situation. Write out your response.

_____

_____

_____

_____

_____

_____

_____

_____

_____

_____

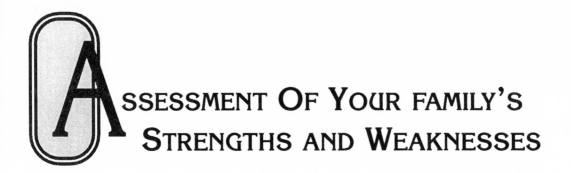

ASSESSMENT OF YOUR FAMILY'S STRENGTHS AND WEAKNESSES

STRENGTHS

Success strategies for helping family members cope with the divorce struggles.

➕ Each individual is able to deal with the feelings they are experiencing.

➕ Family members feel a sense of relief that the long history of conflict is over.

➕ A strong and healthy support system can also make the break-up of the immediate family more palatable. Children and adults can turn to other family friends who are understanding to fill in the emotional gaps.

➕ Children can still maintain relationships with families of both parents.

➕ Family members can minimize fighting and maximize cooperation.

➕ Children learn to turn toward their siblings, and not against them, so they have someone who shares the experience.

➕ Families find ways to reduce stress by continuing to share some fun times together.

WEAKNESSES

Pitfalls to be overcome to learn to deal with the divorce.

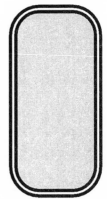

▬ The parents engage in extensive legal battles over everything from kids to cars.

▬ They create an atmosphere of hostility and distrust.

▬ A parent moves a long distance away from the rest of the family.

▬ A parent does not maintain contact or care involvement in the case of the children.

▬ A parent gets involved in another relationship within a few months which disrupts the children's adjustment to the new situation.

COMPLETING YOUR FAMILY ASSESSMENT

An assessment of the strengths and weaknesses of your family should be made as part of the divorce process. Once you know what they are, you will be better able to develop an action plan to help you and your children achieve a successful divorce.

List your family's present strengths and weaknesses for dealing with the divorce. Give specific examples of each.

Strengths

_____
_____
_____
_____
_____
_____
_____
_____

Examples

_____
_____
_____
_____
_____
_____
_____
_____

Weaknesses

_____
_____
_____
_____
_____
_____
_____
_____

Examples

_____
_____
_____
_____
_____
_____
_____
_____

How To Make Your Images A Reality

Now you have gotten an overview of the issues that need to be addressed in order to have a successful divorce. You've also gotten a vision of how your life will be once you have resolved those issues. But how do you get from here to there?

You have already taken the first step. You have begun to educate yourself about how to become successful in an area of life that you previously didn't know much about. Just like in any other endeavor, knowledge is power. You have started off by creating the knowledge that you have a successful life waiting for you in your future.

The second step is to enhance your future vision. This is accomplished in two ways. To begin, you have looked at the six areas of life that need to be satisfied in order for you to have a well balanced life: Body, Mind, Spirit, Work, Love and Play. Then you broke your ultimate goal down into bite-sized "chunks." This gave you an action plan so you knew what to do and when to do it. By having specific steps to follow, you pace yourself and chart your progress as well.

The third step was to look at the needs of everyone in your entire social system. Successful outcomes for people always involve meeting as many  needs as possible for everyone involved in the situation. In this case, that includes yourself, your kid(s), and the children's coparent. It may even include grandparents. What's important to achieving your vision is to recognize that if any of the key players in your life are tremendously unhappy, then they'll try to sabotage you in your efforts to be happy. So you've learned how to create win/win solutions that make everyone happy.

Creating win/win solutions isn't as difficult as it sounds. In fact, generating positive energy can become contagious, effecting all aspects of your life. Things truly do get better once you create your self-fulfilling prophesy for success.

THE TIME MACHINE

Time marches on for your child and yourself. In fact, because children are in the formative time for their development, their lives are more easily shaped than an adult's. Think about what changes you would like to see happen in your child's future. Put your child in the time machine that you've used to see your future, and set the dial for some time in their future. Imagine how your child will have resolved the divorce and gone on to create a good life for themselves. Now write down how your child would describe his or her new life.

PLEDGE/COMMITMENT TO CONTINUING STRENGTHS AND IMPLEMENTING AN ACTION PLAN

One of the tragic consequences of the divorce process is a breakdown of trust between the family members. Your children have always counted on you and your coparent to be together and provide for their needs.

They are concerned that if the bond between their two parents can be broken, so too can the bond which their parents have to them. One way of addressing their concerns is to reassure them of your love for them and to be consistent in your contact and caregiving even if you no longer live in the same house.

It is critically important during this time that you follow through on *any* promises you make to your children. They will be assessing how much they can count on you, so don't blow it now. The consequences to your relationship with your children could be devastating.

Inform your children about the Action Plan which you have developed for helping you both deal with the life changes brought on by the divorce.

Ask for their input and suggestions on how to concentrate on the strengths which each of the members can bring to the process.

Most importantly, establish a commitment that you will work together as a team, encouraging all of the family members to participate in creating a successful divorce.

If your children are able to see that you and your coparent can work together on the Action Plan designed to get through the divorce, they will feel more secure about their future.

Your Family Pledge

Write out a family pledge/commitment with your children which you will follow as you proceed through the divorce process. Once you are satisfied with it, sign it.

I pledge...

_____

_____

_____

_____

_____

_____

_____

_____

_____

_____

_____

Signed by my hand,

_____

Signature

EPILOGUE

Congratulations!! You have now completed your "Hole" basic training program. Now that you are out of the divorce pits, you can see some sunshine again. Even when there are clouds, you'll know that there is a silver lining. For clouds are necessary to bring the rain that helps our flowers grow.

You have learned how to take better care of yourself in the six major areas of your life: Body, Mind, Spirit, Work, Love and Play. And you have helped your children to regain their balance in life as well.

As you continue to work through all the feelings associated with your divorce, you will now realize that you have many choices to keep you from falling back into the "pits".

Conflicts with your coparent had often felt like quicksand when you were stuck and couldn't seem to pull yourself out. Fortunately you have now acquired the tools to avoid those traps. By practicing the **SOLVE** Model, you have taken the steps necessary to empower yourself with a more positive and effective method for communicating and decision-making. This will allow you to brush off all the dirt that covered you when you had fallen into the divorce pit.

You have also earned a "merit badge" for taking the time to learn how the divorce has affected your children. The exercises you have completed have given you insight into how to better help your children avoid being sucked into the "black hole" as well.

Because you have become a more experienced "climber," your children will feel more secure as you guide them through the rugged and often unpredictable terrain of divorce.

Celebrate these steps you have already taken to help your children move on to a HAPPY life. Good luck as you REBUILD your life on solid ground!

We hope this book has been of help to you and we would like to hear from you. Please send us your comments on how this book has helped you. Feel free to add any suggestions you think would make it even better. We will use your feedback in each new edition. Thank you for your help in helping us to help others. We look forward to hearing from you!

Best wishes for a successful new life.

Dr. Thomas Muha   *Dr. Maureen Vernon*

116 Defense Highway, Suite 210A, Annapolis, MD 21401

S O S
SUPPORT & OTHER SERVICES

T he following offer a variety of resources and publications for divorcing parents and their children. Some, such as Parents Without Partners, offer support groups in many communities across the country. Call or write the organizations which most closely appear to meet your needs for more specific information concerning their services and any materials they distribute.

**Association of Family &
Conciliation Courts**
329 W. Wilson St.
Madison, WI 53703
(608)251-4001
Publications

Center for Divorce Education
P.O. Box 5900
Athens, OH 45701
(614)593-1074, 1065
Publications and videotapes

Children's Rights Council
220 Eye St., N.E.
Washington, D.C. 20002
(202)547-6227
Books, audio tapes, newsletter

Joint Custody Association
10606 Wilkins Ave.
Los Angeles, CA 90024
(310)475-5352
Provides information for parents desiring joint custody; assists individuals and groups working for legislative changes

Mothers Without Custody
P.O. Box 27418
Houston, TX 77227-7418
(800)457-6962
Provides emotional support to divorced mothers living apart from their children; send SASE for information and newsletter

**Parents Without Partners
International Office**
8807 Colesville Road
Silver Spring, MD 20910
(301)588-9394
Support groups around the country; publications

Single Parent Resource Center
141 W. 28th Street, Suite 302
New York, NY 10001
(212)947-0221
Referrals to local services and support groups; publications

Stepfamily Association of America
215 Centennial Mall South, Suite 212
Lincoln, NE 68508
(800)735-0329
Books, tapes, manuals; 60 support groups nationwide

To order additional copies of *Divorce Is The Pits,* please fill in the order form below and mail it to the address shown. Please allow 3-4 weeks for delivery. If you wish information on quantity discounts or if you have any other questions, please call 410-263-2000.

Name _____

Address _____

City _____ State_____ Zip _____

Home Phone _____ Work Phone _____

	QUANTITY	PRICE
☐ *Divorce Is The Pits* @ $19.95	_____	_____
☐ *Divorce Is The Pits* Video @ $149.95	_____	_____
☐ Leader's Manual @ $49.95	_____	_____
☐ Therapist's Package: @ $249.95		
7 *Divorce Is The Pits* Books		
1 *Divorce Is The Pits* Video		
1 Leader's Manual	_____	_____
MD residents add 5% sales tax		_____
Shipping total (see below)		_____
TOTAL		_____

SHIPPING, US only
First item (except Therapist's Package) $ 4.95
Each additional item (except Therapist's Package) $ 2.00
Therapist's Package, each $14.95

For shipping outside continental US, please add $ 5.00

☐ Check/Money Order Enclosed   ☐ Charge my: ☐ MasterCard   ☐ VISA

Credit Card No. _____

Exp. Date _____ Signature_____

Mail to:

Looking Glass Productions, Inc.
116 Defense Highway, Ste. 210A, Annapolis, MD 21401
or FAX to 410-266-5537